GRANDCHILD OF EMPIRE

OTHER BOOKS BY
W.H. NEW

Malcolm Lowry (1971)

*Articulating West: Essays on Purpose and Form
in Modern Canadian Literature* (1972)

*Among Worlds: An Introduction to Modern Commonwealth
and South African Literature* (1975)

A Political Art (1978)

*Dreams of Speech and Violence: The Art of the Short Story
in Canada and New Zealand* (1987)

A History of Canadian Literature (1989)

Native Writers and Canadian Writing (1990)

Inside the Poem (1992)

Science Lessons: Poems (1996)

*Land Sliding: Imagining Space, Presence, and
Power in Canadian Writing* (1997)

Borderlands: How We Talk About Canada (1998)

Vanilla Gorilla (1998)

Raucous (1999)

Reading Mansfield and Metaphors of Form (1999)

Stone/Rain (2001)

Llamas in the Laundry (2002)

Encyclopedia of Literature in Canada (2002)

Riverbook & Ocean (2002)

Grandchild *of* Empire

―ಌ

about irony, mainly
in the Commonwealth

THE 2002 GARNETT SEDGEWICK
MEMORIAL LECTURE

W.H. New

RONSDALE PRESS

GRANDCHILD OF EMPIRE
Copyright © 2003 W.H. New

RONSDALE PRESS
3350 West 21st Avenue
Vancouver, B.C., Canada
V6S 1G7

Set in New Baskerville: 11½ pt on 17
Typesetting: Julie Cochrane
Printing: AGMV Marquis, Quebec, Canada
Paper: Rolland "Enviro" — Ancient Forest Free, composed of
    100% post-consumer recycled content with a bleach-free process
Cover Design: Rand Berthaudin & Pause Commun_ications

Ronsdale Press wishes to thank the Canada Council for the Arts, the Government of Canada through the Book Publishing Industry Development Program (BPIDP), and the Province of British Columbia through the British Columbia Arts Council for their support of its publishing program.

National Library of Canada Cataloguing in Publication Data

New, W. H. (William Herbert), 1938–
    Grandchild of empire

    Includes bibliographical references.
    ISBN 1-55380-001-X

    I. Commonwealth literature (English) — History and criticism.
2. Irony in literature. I. Title.
PR9080.N49 2003   820.9'9171241   C2002-910885-3

For Peggy

*And for Sadie Boyles, whose brilliant teaching
influenced my early career, and who was herself
an admiring student of Garnett Sedgewick*

And in memory of my parents

ACKNOWLEDGEMENTS

I WISH TO THANK Sherrill Grace, Head of the Department of English at the University of British Columbia, for the invitation to deliver the 2002 Sedgewick Lecture, and my colleagues for their friendship and support. Especially I am grateful to Laurie Ricou, Patricia Lackie, Margaret Tom-Wing, and Dominique Yupangco for organizing the occasion, and Ronald Hatch for bringing this lecture so elegantly into printed form. I am indebted, too, to the following owners of copyrighted material for their permission to reprint it here: I.B.H. Publishing Co., Canada Post, Little Brown & Co., Dave Coverly & Creators Syndicate, Inc., and Len Peterson. Every reasonable effort has been made to find copyright holders. The publisher would be pleased to have any errors or omissions brought to its attention.

—๏ Introduction

The Sedgewick Lectures are named in honour of Garnett G. Sedgewick, who was the founding Head of the Department of English at the University of British Columbia, and the first Lecture was given in 1955 (six years after his death). Over the years many distinguished scholars and writers have given the Sedgewick lecture — among them Harry Levin, Hugh Mac-Lennan, Northrop Frye, Robert Bringhurst, Anne McClintock, and last year Jonathan Goldberg.

This year's Sedgewick Lecturer is Dr. William H. New, UBC University Killam Professor and one of the University's and Canada's most distinguished scholars. It is a very special privilege and honour to introduce Dr. New — whom we know more familiarly as "Bill" — because he is one of our own and because it is only on rare occasions that this prestigious lecture is given by a member of our own Department. Bill New, who joined UBC in 1965, is a specialist in the areas of Canadian and Commonwealth (more commonly known today as Postcolonial) literatures; indeed, over his long and distinguished career he has been a shaping force in both fields. He is a Fellow of the Royal Society of Canada and has won many awards and prizes including the Jacob Biely Prize and the UBC Killam prizes for research and for teaching. From 1995-97 he held the Brenda and David McLean Chair in Canadian Studies at UBC.

From 1977 to 1995 he served as Editor of the scholarly journal *Canadian Literature,* which is the leading journal in the field. Under his guiding hand and eye the journal became internationally celebrated and carried innovative research on Canada and Canadian literature around the world. But Bill's contributions to the study of literature extend far beyond this important work. He has published well over three hundred articles, chapters, editorials, and reviews, authored twelve scholarly books, and edited many more. Among these books are foundational works on Canadian literary history — *A History of Canadian Literature* (1989) or *Land Sliding: Imagining Space, Presence, and Power in Canadian Writing* (1997) — and on particular New Zealand, Australian, and Canadian writers — *Dreams of Speech and Violence: The Art of the Short Story in Canada and New Zealand* (1987) or *Reading Mansfield and Metaphors of Form* (1999). His mammoth editorial enterprise — the *Encyclopedia of Literature in Canada* — is forthcoming from the University of Toronto Press later this year, and it signifies the kind of extraordinary knowledge, scope, and scholarly generosity that characterizes the career of this man.

But Bill New can by no means be summed up by his scholarship alone. He is an award-winning teacher, a mentor to generations of graduate students who now teach and conduct their research in universities around the world. He is a generous and thoughtful colleague, an avid gardener, a deft squash player, a wit (whose wry, punning sense of humour is never far from the surface), and a poet. Perhaps it is in this last mentioned capacity — as poet — where we can see his scholarly love for literature blurring with and feeding into his passion for language, rhythm, imagery, and communication. He has already five books of poetry to his credit, with two more forthcoming! As someone recently asked: can there really be only ONE Bill New? The answer, I suspect, may be found in the poem called "Being Only" from his first volume for children, *Vanilla Gorilla*:

> I feel like hidden treasure
> That is hoarded in a sieve —
> It's really very hard to hide
> Where Only Children live —
>
> So if one day I have the chance
> To be my opposite,
> I'd like to live as triplets
> Just to share the load a bit.

The 2002 Sedgewick Lecture is one more indication of Bill New's talents. *Grandchild of Empire: about irony, mainly in the Commonwealth,* brings together his knowledge of literature, his love of ideas, his passion for language (its double entendres, its marvellous ambiguities, its rich associations), and his ability to perform, something the written version of the lecture can only hint at. In performance, the New triplets addressed us in literary voices from around and about the world.

Sherrill Grace
Professor and Head, Dept. of English, UBC
February 2002

—⌒ *I. About Definition*

I would like to begin by thanking my colleagues for inviting
me to give the 2002 Sedgewick lecture. It is a privilege and an
honour. Garnett Sedgewick was known as a particularly
gifted teacher and a fine scholar; and the title of his book, *Of
Irony, especially in drama,*[1] provides a kind of tangential start to
my talk today, *about irony, mainly in the Commonwealth.* Tangential because what I want to do is partly personal — to take the
chance to pay tribute to my own teachers, and to the art of
teaching *indirectly.* Partly, too, because this talk is a critical
exercise not just in examining inheritance and imitation but
also in the art of indirection. *About* irony: the lead preposi-
tion in my title hints at a *non-*linear challenge: so I will be
non-linear in what I have to say, by intention. *About:* from OE
onbutan, "on the outside." I do not want simply to repeat what
critics and theorists have said about irony in general,[2] but to
look at what some specific literary examples suggest about
the function of subject, strategy, and tone. I want to refer
both to some issues in colonial social history and to some
techniques of writing in the Commonwealth that are related
to them. And I want to talk about some of the ways in which
irony functions, not just as a humorous device (which it often

is) or as a way of troping dismissal (which it all too often can be), but as a voice of resistance to authority *and at the same time* as a covert affirmation of some of the intricate ways in which the generations of Empire and Independence relate.

As a literary technique irony is conventionally defined as "saying one thing but meaning another," a riddling phrase (see Ill. 1) that not only calls to mind what Alice almost said

The engineer says he got orders to build in both Hindi and English—and that he knows both!

Ill. 1: Laxman (R.K. Narayan's brother) was one of India's foremost political and social cartoonists. This ironic view of post-independence language policy was collected in Laxman's You Said It #3, *published by I.B.H. Publishing Co., Bombay, 1968.*

to the March Hare[3] (that she says what she means and means
what she says) but also sounds as much like justifying a mis-
taken word choice as a conscious rhetorical strategy. One of
the many ironies of irony, perhaps. Yet it is not quite accurate
to restrict irony this way, for irony often means saying what
you mean at a slant, or saying two things at once — *oversetting:*
so that a reader might hear (through the *performance* of a
given set of words) not only their split levels of *implication* but
also the divergent *relation* between an apparent surface
intent and an often political undertow.[4] "Voice," writes the
poet Lisa Robertson, "is a hybrid of the sonic and the political."[5] This blur between *saying* and *meaning* creates a sort of
rhetorical diversion, a pause while meaning and function can
be figured out; and often the figuring out occurs in an act
of recognition (or, as D.J. Enright has it, "reverberation") —
rather than in an act of explanation — which means that
irony, to be effective, depends upon context and shared
knowledge. So let me set up here a context both personal
and social, so that I can then go on to probe the literary politics of Imperial Centre and Commonwealth margin — and
vice-versa — and then circle back to the ordinariness (not the
exoticism) that irony persistently reads.

—ᐤ II. About Empire and Commonwealth

When I was about eleven years old, I went home from school one afternoon with what I thought then was one of the best jokes I'd ever heard, one that I saved securely in my head so that I could tell it at the kitchen table. It went something like this: An English gent had been staying for a week at the Waldorf Astoria hotel in New York when a local man came up to him and asked him if he liked riddles. When the Englishman said yes, the American said: "Well, then, here's a riddle for you: 'Sisters and brothers have I none, and yet this man is my father's son: Who is it?'" "I say," said the Englishman, "that's a puzzle. I don't know: who is it?" "Hah," said the American; "it's me!" "Jolly good," said the Englishman; "I must tell that at my club when I return to London." So in due course he does go home, and at his club one day the Englishman says, "I say, I have a riddle from America. It goes like this: 'Sisters and brothers have I none, and yet this man is my father's son: Who is it?'" "I say," reply the clubmen, "that's jolly difficult: who is it?" "Why," says the Englishman, "it's the man in the Waldorf Astoria."

The joke works, of course, to the degree that it does, because of how it uses some of the strategies of comic writing:

ordinary premise, twisted logic, voice, pacing, repetition, and punchline. I also think it works *in Canada* because its central figures — the Yank and the English Old Boy — are caricatures of two presumptuous Empires to which Canadians not-so-secretly feel superior and beside which they nevertheless so often, so hungrily, graze. Fairly clearly, the voice is that of irony; it belongs to an observer who shares with his listeners a dimension of both unease and understanding, that gives them, together, a kind of freedom from whatever authority the caricatures in the story, whether blatant or not, obliquely represent. I remember this joke, however, for other, much more personal reasons. When I told it at supper, everyone laughed — except my father, who after a short pause said, "I don't get it." And everyone laughed again. He did, of course, "get it," but he was indirectly teaching me something else, with an irony of his own, about the rhetoric of dissent; for years after, whenever any of us ran up against a bureaucratic failure to understand, all we had to say was "the man in the Waldorf Astoria" for another gale of laughter to set us free.

Let me tell you a little about my father. He was born, at the turn of the last century, in what was then a small town in a far corner of northwest India. It's an ordinary story, not an exotic one, though for a long time I thought otherwise. My British Army grandfather had gone there some years earlier — and that is more or less the limit of my knowledge of Victorian family history. So in some ways I am a grandchild of Empire. I grew up hearing stories of India in my grand-father's house; I learned to count in Hindustani at about the same time as in English; and I suspect that I could trace my ongoing fascination with the modern literatures of the Commonwealth to this early endorsement of the subcontinent's cultural vigour.

Today, writers such as Salman Rushdie argue that the Commonwealth is itself a political and historical irony — or aberration — an organization born of economics and competitive nationalism as much as anything, which secretly preserves the footprints of imperial power, and is therefore, in Rushdie's view, an inadequate basis for any term describing innovative art. This position leads Rushdie into a sweeping, easy, and illogical dismissal of "Commonwealth literature," because, he says, "Commonwealth literature" is a monolithic hegemonic box into which he will not be stuffed.[6] Whatever else, his dismissal is a deliberately provocative gesture that manages to be both politically correct and arch-conservative. For Rushdie chooses in his essay not to find out if the singular box actually existed in the first place. The answer to this unasked question is of course No, it didn't: at least, it didn't among any *critical* readers of the plural English-language literatures of the Commonwealth, for they have long been as interested in the features and implications of diversity as much as they are in those of similarity, overlap, and connection.

And yet, what Rushdie may fundamentally be responding to — like the novelist and poet Zulfikar Ghose, in a later essay, who notes that the "Commonwealth" label confined him but gave him advantages at the same time — are the metaphors that underlie various attempts to use a singular definition of Commonwealth and Empire, and to construct a simple linear version of literary history to include, explain, and then *explain away* "Commonwealth" writers and writing *as marginal.* Ghose, now a Texas resident, complains that "Commonwealth" literature has been read only for its exoticism and not for its quality — an interesting premise: although (like Rushdie, who insists that there is only one English literature, because English is a world language, and that he is a world writer) he leaves the word "quality" undefined, thus opening up another mixed box of absolutes and uncertainties.[7] Enthusiasts for the linear paradigm — those who implicitly saw Britain as the source and model, and the USA as the brightest reflective star — concocted attractive but unworkable ways of troping colonial and postcolonial cultures: the branches of the tree, the daughters of the queen-mother, the fragments in the glass, all implicitly *lesser.* The point about metaphors is that they have the power to make us see things in a particular way, and of course once we see them that way we sometimes have to free ourselves from the metaphor in order to understand how in some loose sense we're being politically constrained. This insight is one of the less happy conclusions to draw from P.K. Page's "Cook's Mountains," a poem about Captain Cook naming what are now known as the Glasshouse Mountains in Queensland, and which reads in part:

> By naming them he made them.
> They were there
> before he came
> but they were not the same.
> It was his gaze
> that glazed each one.

It is *his glass* that sees the "glasshouse" mountains; they "shine" as they do because "his tongue" is "silvered with paradox and metaphor."[8]

What's wrong with metaphors of simple colonial reflection is more or less the same thing that the Cherokee-German-Greek-American-Canadian writer Thomas King rails against in "Godzilla vs. Post-Colonial."[9] As King makes clear, the term "postcolonial" (which has largely replaced "Commonwealth" in much recent commentary) is not free from the rumble of political assumption and political desire. The chronological linearity suggested by one reading of the *post* in "postcolonial," King affirms — like the limited authority granted the branch/daughter/fragment figures — implicitly assumes a hierarchical relation between here and there, near and far, now and then. In the case of aboriginal peoples, "postcolonial" (in King's reading of the term) also suggests that there was no *pre-colonial,* no culture or cultures in place prior to the arrival of English (or French, or any other European language) to which contemporary people might look back with pride or on whose integrity they might in some measure continue rewardingly to draw. Like P.K. Page's Captain Cook in Queensland, the imperial language *un-names* even as it names anew.

But just as the un-naming of the Other constitutes a dangerous temptation for many writers and critics, there is a second danger in assuming the existence of a perfect world prior to colonization. As Homi Bhabha has argued,[10] diversity is the real norm in the world, even within cultures like that of "the English" or "the French," who sometimes pretend to uniformity; and all societies are imperfect.[11] Yet a third danger arises from assuming that to *recognize* difference is to act even-handedly. I am not talking absence of evaluation here: everyone evaluates, all the time. But simply to *recognize* difference does not automatically free people from the hierarchies of authority that they conventionally grant to relationships and repeatedly build into comparisons between the familiar (or that which some assumed authority has made familiar) and whatever else exists that the familiar makes strange. Such an environment is both fraught with irony and ripe for it.

—꙰ III. About History: a digression

The "British Commonwealth" (later, the Commonwealth of Nations, dropping "British") came into existence in 1931, in the wake of the Balfour Report of 1926,[12] and after the Statute of Westminster had worked out some of the details of inter-nation relationship that would inevitably follow the devolution of Empire. A previous notion called "Imperial Federation," promoted during the latter part of the nineteenth century, had envisioned an Imperial parliament, to which Australia, Canada, New Zealand, Cape Colony, and the United Kingdom would send representatives, but this idea (championed by the Canadian writer Sara Jeannette Duncan, among others) failed to appeal to those who actually held political power at the time, and failed also to grant any kind of representation to the non-settler sectors of the Empire. As established in 1931, the Commonwealth was still hierarchical, for it still involved only Britain and three of the four settler societies, and left out the Empire's non-European member states. New Zealand, cautious about social change, refused to fully endorse entering the Commonwealth until 1947 — not wanting, in their leaders' words, to weaken the bonds of Empire. The conventional "red map" of Britain's Empire circling the globe–on which, as the slogan had it, the

Ill. 2: This Mercator projection of the British Empire was reproduced on classroom wall maps throughout the Commonwealth well into the 1950s; in this version it exaggerates Canada's centrality and relative size. The image of the Canadian stamp is reproduced courtesy of Canada Post.

sun never set[13] (see Ill. 2) — could thus remain intact for a few more decades.

After South Asian societies regained their independence in 1947, however — though in a different form from that which they had held prior to contact with Britain — changes in Imperial and Commonwealth structure began more rapidly to take effect. Among other things, some newly enfranchised nations (Burma, for one) chose not to join the Commonwealth; others (e.g., Pakistan) left, subsequently to rejoin; some (South Africa, Fiji) temporarily withdrew or were suspended from the Commonwealth by the Commonwealth secretariat, but rejoined or were reinstated later after their social policies had been reformed; others endorsed alternative governmental models: India chose to be a republic rather than a constitutional monarchy within the Commonwealth arrangement, Tonga to retain its own monarch while still acknowledging the British crown as head of state within the Commonwealth.

Still other political and social changes took place within individual nations. For example, Canadian citizenship legislation (passed in 1946, enacted in 1947) was the first in the Empire/Commonwealth to alter the implicitly colonial designation of citizenship that had existed to this time. Until 1947, that is, all Commonwealth citizens were declared to be "British subjects" on their passports, which tacitly granted them access both to Britain and to British law. When in 1946 Mackenzie King's government in Ottawa passed the new legislation, "Canadian citizenship" acquired precedence over "British subject" for both immigrants and the native-born alike. While the phrase "A Canadian citizen is a British subject" remained on Canadian passports, as a secondary designation, for years to come, the Canadian Citizenship Act of 1970 — along with Britain's altered priorities, with its entry into the Common Market — changed numerous conventions such as these. In the late 1940s, moreover, with India and Pakistan now in the Commonwealth, and in light of the Commonwealth agreement that member states were equal to each other, the Canadian government belatedly granted voting rights to its citizens of South Asian heritage.

A table to show the devolution of Empire and the growth of the Commonwealth (to 54 nations by 2002) will indicate the speed of this process of change:

ABOUT IRONY, MAINLY IN THE COMMONWEALTH

DATE OF INDEPENDENCE	NATION	DATE OF JOINING THE COMMONWEALTH
1776	13 colonies of the USA (expanded to its current size over the next two centuries, with Alaska and Hawaii achieving statehood in 1959)	never in the Commonwealth
1867	Canada (the former colonies of Upper and Lower Canada, Nova Scotia, and New Brunswick joining in "Confederation," as the "Dominion of Canada"; with subsequent colonies joining, as "provinces," during the decades to come: Manitoba in 1870, British Columbia in 1871, Prince Edward Island in 1873, Alberta and Saskatchewan in 1905, Newfoundland & Labrador in 1949; Yukon and Rupert's Land (as the "Northwest Territories") were joined to the Dominion in 1870, with Yukon created as a separate territory in 1898, and Nunavut in 2001)	1931
1901	Australia (federating, as the Commonwealth of Australia, the states of Queensland, New South Wales, Victoria, South Australia, and Western Australia, with Northern Territory granted to Australia in 1911)	1931
1907	New Zealand	as an observer, 1931; formally in 1947
1910	South Africa (the Union of South Africa uniting the Cape of Good Hope Colony and Natal with the Boer Republics of Orange Free State and	1931-1961; rejoined 1994

DATE OF INDEPENDENCE	NATION	DATE OF JOINING THE COMMONWEALTH
1910	Transvaal; later called Republic of South Africa)	
1937	Irish Free State (later Eire, the Irish Republic)	not in the Commonwealth
1947	India	1947
	Pakistan	1947; withdrew 1972, rejoined 1989; suspended from Commonwealth councils 1999
1948	Burma (later Myanmar)	not in the Commonwealth
	Sri Lanka (formerly Ceylon)	1948
1957	Ghana (uniting the colonies of Gold Coast and Togoland)	1957
	Malaysia (Malaya, joining with Sarawak and North Borneo as the Federation of Malaysia in 1963)	1957
1960	Cyprus	1961
	Nigeria	1960
1961	Sierra Leone	1961
	Tanganyika (joining with Zanzibar to become Tanzania in 1964)	1961
1962	Jamaica	1962
	Trinidad & Tobago	1962
	Uganda	1962
	Western Samoa (as Samoa)	1970
1963	Kenya	1963
1964	Malawi (formerly Nyasaland)	1964

ABOUT IRONY, MAINLY IN THE COMMONWEALTH

DATE OF INDEPENDENCE	NATION	DATE OF JOINING THE COMMONWEALTH
1964	Malta	1964
	Zambia (formerly Northern Rhodesia)	1964
1965	The Gambia	1965
	Maldives	1982
	Singapore	1965
1966	Barbados	1966
	Botswana (formerly Bechuanaland)	1966
	Guyana (formerly British Guiana)	1966
	Lesotho (formerly Basutoland)	1966
1968	Mauritius	1968
	Nauru	1968
	Swaziland	1968
1970	Fiji	1970-1987; rejoined 1997
	Tonga	1970
1971	Bangladesh (separating from Pakistan)	1972
1973	The Bahamas	1973
1974	Grenada	1974
1975	Papua New Guinea	1975
1976	Seychelles	1976
1978	Dominica	1978
	Solomon Islands	1978
	Tuvalu (formerly Ellice Islands)	1978
1979	Kiribati (formerly Gilbert Islands)	1979

DATE OF INDEPENDENCE	NATION	DATE OF JOINING THE COMMONWEALTH
1979	St Lucia	1979
	St Vincent & The Grenadines	1979
	Zimbabwe (formerly Southern Rhodesia, which had unilaterally declared independence in 1965)	1980
1980	Vanuatu (formerly New Hebrides)	1980
1981	Antigua & Barbuda	1981
	Belize (formerly British Honduras)	1981
1983	St Christopher (St Kitts) & Nevis	1983
1984	Brunei Darussalam	1984
1990	Namibia (formerly South West Africa)	1990

In 1995, Cameroun (which was created in 1982 from the former British and French Cameroons) and Mozambique (which had achieved independence from Portugal in 1976) also joined the Commonwealth, seeking the economic, educational, and political opportunities that by this time the organization provided. Insofar as French and Portuguese (rather than English) were the dominant "European" languages used in these states, another stage in the historical transformation of the Commonwealth had thus been reached. Definitions of "Commonwealth literature" also changed, for the presumed commonality of the English language no longer provided a ready boundary.[14] The move in literary criticism — towards "postcolonial literatures" (in the plural) — gathered momentum.

During this long process, the devolution of Empire was

not uniformly praised. Many people in Britain — writers, politicians, ordinary citizens — read it as "loss": loss of possessions, loss of status, loss of glory. Even in the former colonies, some writers and other people shared in this attitude — partly because they had accepted their affiliation with imperial force or display (wealth, opulence, majesty) as a vicarious hold upon power and a palliative to their identity as "colonial." To those who identified with Empire, losing any sign of apparent precedence implied a commensurate loss of personal prestige. Likewise, at the so-called heart of Empire, "displacement" from the accustomed role as world ruler (whether real or imagined) was hard for some people to deal with psychologically. The idea of "equality" perhaps especially grated wherever class distinctions had been assumed to be an acceptable norm.

But the Empire was turning into Commonwealth whether such people found it palatable or not, and political change had to be dealt with. Characteristically, however, the new relationship among nations (like the old) was represented in family terms, and the ironies of identity in an exhausted postwar "Britain" are nowhere more apparent than in a 1948 cartoon by the British artist David Low at the time of the Commonwealth Prime Ministers' Conference in London. (See Ill. 3) It depicts Mother England and her Colonial Children, who have finally come of age and at last acquired their own house keys; "Mother," somewhat wistfully, is asking if anyone minds if she keeps one key herself. The irony is perhaps a way to accept the inevitability of a shift in power, but it doesn't admit to liking it. In fact it hints that attitudes to

Ill. 3: David Low's 1948 cartoon, depicting Britannia as "Mother,"
suggests the ambivalence of British attitudes at the time to the whole idea of
"Commonwealth." The cartoon is reprinted here from Atlas of the British
Empire, *ed. Christopher Bayly (New York: Facts on File Press, 1989).*
Courtesy of Little Brown & Co.

power, centre, and periphery were continuing — among at least some Britons — largely unchanged. To cast the "former colonies" as nations "equal in stature" to their own was seemingly beyond their imaginative reach, whether they were aristocrats, ordinary people, or politicians. Training in the discourse of precedence and hierarchy died hard.[15] To cast the so-called colonies as children, by contrast, perpetuated the infantilizing conventions of previous centuries' worth of political expansion. As the Low cartoon reveals, using whimsy to depict new-nation claims on status was a way of simultaneously accepting the reality of postwar political diminishment and refusing the morality of devolution. Using a rhetoric of dismissal permitted those who used it to continue to feel superior, whatever their actual lives might tell them.

Elleke Boehmer makes the point that these attitudes were already evident in the inter-war period, especially in the work of such writers as Graham Greene, Evelyn Waugh, Joyce Cary, and others who — in travel writing and comedies of Englishmen abroad —

> were self-conscious and parodic inheritors of the Boy's Own type of narrative. They proclaimed its obsolescence, lampooning stereotyped styles and poses. And yet . . . [t]heir cynical antics bec[a]me a form of wistful retrospection, once again suggesting an unwillingness or an inability to change. Seemingly, in a world disturbingly prone to cataclysm, there was self-protection to be found in irony. . . . In the late imperial context . . . irony could work as a support for, as well as scourge of, imperial stasis. . . . [It] was favoured . . . because it tended to reproduce rather than to upturn existing structures in the world.[16]

Just so. But an important distinction to be made here is that between irony as the rhetoric of an exhausted withdrawal from action (or acceptance of change) and irony as a process that promotes and participates in social and political reform. Postwar irony, that is, did not just work to protect the past; it also turned to look directly at social upheaval. England became the subject of former colonial writers abroad as well as the other way round. Trinidad-born Samuel Selvon, for example, in *The Lonely Londoners* (1956), writes that

> A lot of the men get kill in war and leave widow behind, and it have bags of these old geezers who does be pottering about

the Harrow Road like if they lost, a look in their eye as if the war happen unexpected and they still can't realise what happen to the old Brit'n.[17]

Even Selvon's discourse patterns function politically here: they disrupt the received conventions of literariness. In the orality of his style, one of the voices of what had been the margin becomes a centre in its own right.

There came to be a divide, therefore, between those writers who hung on to a discourse that articulated the ideology of empire (as though by using it they could deny the reality of imperial devolution) and those who used a discourse of relocation, opposition, or deconstruction: those who placed their allegiance in independence, in their own voice (even at home in Britain),[18] and in the figurative language that emerged from their own locale. For these latter writers, irony functioned as a strategy of dismissal: a covert reply to imperial presumptuousness and racist ridicule. Poems such as Edward Lucie-Smith's "Imperialists in Retirement" or Derek Walcott's "Ruins of a Great House" might cast a sympathetic eye on the *effects* of loss on former "masters," but they do not wish the masters back, nor regret political change.

In other words, such change did not take place without political incident, nor without literary effect. But nor did it always represent "progress." To the degree that America became a substitute social model, in many Commonwealth states, replacing Mother England, "dependence" translated into another politics, a further set of received images, a cultural rhetoric of monetary value, military power, and technological advance, and a new fashion for mimicry of mass-market style. In Edward Brathwaite's *The Arrivants,* therefore, poetics and politics coincide: the zoot-suited strutting image of the black man in Jamaica, says the poem, must be displaced before self-esteem can be realized. And as with the quest for nationhood, self-esteem had to be cultivated as well as claimed.

Why irony turned out to be a strategy of such cultivation — a route towards self-esteem — is another question. To answer it one has to return to the differences between a colony of settlers and a colony of subjugated peoples, but also to appreciate the relation between the two. Within post-colonial theory, political terms are almost always in dispute, but conventional usage applies the term "First World" fairly consistently to Europe and the USA, "Second World" to such "settler" nations as Canada and Australia, and "Third World" to the newly independent, post-imperial nations of Asia and Africa (and sometimes also to racialized and marginalized groups within the "first" and "second" worlds). "Fourth World" (though the term "First Nations" reconstrues this as an alternative First World) refers to the indigenous cultures that persisted inside settler societies. The numerical system in use here creates its own problems, the whiff of hierarchy being one of them. But the dialogue between politics and rhetoric complicates this easy artifice.

A recurrent critical question asks: Can postcoloniality apply in any circumstances except those of the "Third" world? Most post-colonial (*with* the hyphen) commentary tends to say no, whether by direct statement or by privileging questions of Third World marginalization and the poetics and politics of ethnic and racial categories. Yet in practice, critics sometimes use postcolonial theory to address questions of sexual preference, gender, region, authenticity, and indigeneity as well, and to the degree that these additional categories blur the meaning of "postcoloniality," the nascent taxonomy that divides Third from Second World — as literary categories — breaks down.

Any implied equation between the "Settler/Subjugated" paradigm and the "Second/Third World" paradigm has also to be recognized as inaccurate in detail, for none of these categories is classless or uniform, although some of the assumptions that lie behind the distinction "Settler/Subjugated" are nevertheless open to analysis. Among these assumptions are those that derive from any given society's social values. How these are established sets up still more questions: What priority, for example, does a society attach to ancestral rights and property rights? to occupation and ownership? to claim and displacement, movement by force or necessity and movement by free choice? to identification by means of exile and identification with reference to home? to centrality or marginality, colour, gender, language, belief and general access to opportunity? Whatever pattern emerges from answers to these questions will spell out a society's organization and — in a very general way — affect and contextualize its literary culture.

Obviously Third World and Second World experiences are not identical; Jamaica does differ from Australia, Zimbabwe from New Zealand. Societies that champion individualism, moreover, differ from those that privilege communal

values or collectivities, while still other societies seek to nego-
tiate balances between the one and the many, shaping specific
systems of social organization to bring about their particular
version of a workable state. Obviously, too, a *poetics* of resistance is not the same as a *politics* of resistance-in-action;
hence, for example, Aboriginal political protest in Australia
differs in kind as well as in impact from social comment in
Australian literary magazines. Yet there remains a connection between political ends and literary techniques. Edward
Brathwaite's critique of self-denigration and self-reaffirma-
tion are possible everywhere, and the rhetoric of literary
protest *can* resonate beyond the specific circumstances to
which it refers.

—⟋ IV. About Theory, History, and Transformation

How does theory deal with this tension between the specific and the general, and what does it have to do with irony? As Stephen Slemon makes clear — acknowledging the powerful appeal of the categorical division between Third and Second Worlds, in "Unsettling the Empire: Resistance Theory for the Second World"[19] — resistance cannot be simply equated with an experiential category, nor can anti-colonialist measures be seen as the prerogative only of those who declare they feel most marginalized. The settler societies of the so-called Second World (in Australia and Canada, say) — because they, too, constitute sites of radical ambivalence in social experience — can therefore contribute productively to a post-colonial cultural debate, provided they listen as well as speak. Slemon's focus, in consequence, usefully falls on the *condition* of settler-society cultures, and therefore on both politics and the means through which political ideologies are normalized, disputed, reconfigured, and challenged again. In other words, he argues that the idea of "home" — the state we separately identify as "ours" — is itself a version of "norm," and is consequently as much a textual phenomenon (an

34

agreement in words) as it is a temporal or spatial claim on territory. By this reasoning, "imperial" cultures are those that act as though the norms of language and the social priorities that language articulates were fixed. To challenge this assumption, post-imperial cultures, by contrast, reconstitute themselves through a variety of — loosely speaking — "textual" coping strategies, such as opposition, confrontation, mimicry, irony, and polemic. So-called "direct" statement is only "direct" within a particular textual and cultural frame, (see Ill. 4) leaving "indirect" strategies to do the slow work of attitudinal reform. Irony, moreover — a site of radical ambivalence in rhetoric or poetics — deals both with the condition of culture and with the condition of language. The aim is not just reform but also attitudinal *transformation,* for the self who speaks as well as among others who might only look on. But because irony is an implicitly oral as well as a textual medium, it has to be "heard," and heard in context, which affects the reading or listening strategies that go by such names as "reception" and "interpretation."

Listening is made an even more complicated act because the multiple social contexts for postcolonial literatures are both general and specific. The *general* reasons for the establishment of the colonies in the first place, of course, were both political and economic. They had to do with the rise of European nationalism (and the concomitant transfer of power from Church authorities to State authorities); they drew on a received equation between land ownership (or rule) and power; and they presumed that the world's resources should increase wealth among the class that ruled at

Ill. 4: This syndicated "Speedbump" cartoon first appeared in 2000. It overlays the contemporary anti-drinking campaign phrase "designated driver" on a conventional image (parodied in Frank Moorehouse's "The Drover's Wife," among other stories) of the sheep-herder's close relation with his sheep. Reprinted by permission of Dave Coverly and Creators Syndicate, Inc.

the Empire's centre. While the *specific* reasons for the establishment of individual colonies were sometimes simply opportunistic (though often declared to be altruistic), always they had to do with ways of applying whatever were the received beliefs in political and economic command. The transportation of convicts to Australia, for example (after the American Revolution in 1776 made transportation to Virginia impossible), was an economic decision; the practice was cheaper than jailing convicts at home. The granting of half-pay and land in Canada to demobilized soldiers (which led to John and Susanna Moodie emigrating to Upper Canada in the 1830s) was part of a strategy to reduce the size of the British army in the wake of the Napoleonic Wars — and therefore again a government tactic to save money. Sometimes the reasons for colonial expansion were ostensibly scientific, sectarian, and military. The desire to control shipping passage, as for example in Egypt or the Straits of Malacca, led to one form of occupation. The will to convert people from one faith to another led to a second. Those who occupied the military fortifications, however, did not usually honour the cultures in place around them; and those who established the mission colonies often collected or destroyed the artifacts of rituals that their conventional faith did not respect.

But the primary reasons for European national expansion were economic: a consequence of technological and industrial change, which served the manufacturing process and the temporality of successive fashions (fur for the beaver hat, silk and cotton for the fabric mills). An increasing demand for foodstuffs and other commodities also served expansion.

Among these resources (refashioned into "products") were fish, spices, sugar, butter — the last of which was made into a possible import from the South Pacific when nineteenth-century refrigeration made long distance shipping of perishable goods possible. Other products included the minerals that served industrialization and privilege itself: gold, silver, diamonds, copper, coal. What is left out of these lists are the actual lives of the individual people that such enterprises corralled into service, and the disparities of power that resulted from them. Some people (mostly men) held power and opportunity within the distribution system; others claimed it; still others had it taken from them or summarily denied.

For while the list of commodities does not include people, people were clearly treated as commodities. (In some instances they still are: as in the West African chocolate trade as recently as 2001.) Spanish rhetoric in the sixteenth and seventeenth centuries, for example, spoke of the slaves who were collected and sold to serve the sugar trade not in numbers of persons but in terms of "tonnage," and the impression that this rhetorical trope gives is reinforced by the hard data that slave trade history records.[20] The Spanish slave trade in Africa, to take a particular example, began in earnest in 1501, after the Borgia pope Alexander VI in 1494 drew an arbitrary line in the Americas to divide the "new world" between Spain and Portugal. (The doctrine of *terra nullius* — declaring that aboriginal territories were "no-one's land" — had later parallels in Australia and elsewhere.) By 1549 more than 100,000 Africans had been taken to the Western hemisphere — bought and sold as "imports." Of these, three in ten died on the voyage, during the "Middle Passage" (the trip from Africa to the Caribbean, as distinct from the first leg of the ships' journey, from Europe to Africa, or the third, which took sugar cane and other products to Europe to be refined).[21] "Slave plantations" on the island of Barbuda, moreover, deliberately constructed slave-breeding facilities, and so furthered the dehumanizing process. Large areas of Angola and Mozambique were effectively depopulated. Over the next three centuries, the number of Africans sold into slavery in the Americas increased drastically as Portugal, England, France, and the Netherlands joined in the *trade* (the word itself emphasizes the commodity economy). Slavery was also introduced into American cotton plantations in 1619, and by the eighteenth century over 100,000 men, women, and children were taken annually from Guinea alone. When opposition mounted against these practices, the slave trade was abolished, but slowly: by Denmark in 1803, Britain in 1807 (though existing slaves were not freed in British territories till the Emancipation Act in 1833), Spain in 1820, Sweden in 1846, France in 1848, Holland and the USA in 1863, Puerto Rico in 1873, and Cuba in 1880.

English opposition to emancipation during the early nineteenth century rested mainly in the House of Lords, because the Earl of Westmoreland, the Duke of Clarence, Earl St Vincent, Baron Rodney, Lord Nelson — and others, such as the novelist Matthew ("Monk") Lewis — were all West Indies absentee planters and traders in slaves. But post-slavery conditions in the Caribbean did not immediately resolve the disparities that slavery had established, just as the social disparities related to race within the USA (or Canada) were not immediately addressed by the Civil War or the Emancipation Act. Indeed, the indentured labour system that British colonial policy endorsed after 1839 created further social disparities in and among the former colonies. Drawing on the long-standing connection between land ownership, gender, and the right to exert effective political influence on social policy, it established a particular form of capitalism as the working economic principle of the new social order. The so-called "free labour" policy that was introduced on the Caribbean sugar plantations after 1833, for example, involved the hiring of the former slaves to work the plantations — but they were then charged fees for the little housing and food that were accessible to them, *and also for lessons in the work ethic, in how to do the plantation work that they had already been required to do under the previous system.* After fees had been deducted from wages, moreover, these "free" labourers had little money left with which to buy the land to which they now ostensibly had access, and which in theory would be the basis for some more tangible form of independence and freedom. Unable to move, they therefore stayed in place; so did the plantation system, for many years to come.

Slaves, former slaves, former slave-owners, and middle-class reformers all responded to such conditions differently. Some slaves, for example, deliberately committed suicide rather than endure captivity at all; others devised strategies of personal and physical survival, such as the dance called the limbo, which was first performed as exercise in the cramped, low-ceilinged conditions on board the slave ships. Other responses were political and military. From the sixteenth through the nineteenth centuries, for instance, countless slave rebellions took place in the Americas; while most of them were quelled, some did lead to the parlous independence of Haiti, and to the free "maroon" (from *cimarron,* "wild") communities that developed in the limestone mountains of central Jamaica. From these resistance efforts, too, emerged some of the black communities in Nova Scotia and some of those of present-day equatorial Africa.[22] People whom the governors of the West Indian colonies found troublesome were sometimes "relocated" to colonial Canada; and especially after humanitarian anti-slavery movements had gathered momentum, the British and American governments decided (unfortunately without cultural insight or adequate planning) to establish "homeland" communities of "returned slaves" in Sierra Leone and Liberia.

Fundamentally, all these resistance efforts were attitudinal. They were concerned with mental survival as well as physical, the refusal of conditions that inhibited self-esteem. And they had literary consequences. Adapting folktale to comment on existing conditions was one strategy that storytellers employed in the Caribbean; song was another effective literary medium; the slave narrative was a third. (Given the devotion to class structure that otherwise marks her work, it is noteworthy that Susanna Moodie was very much involved in anti-slavery causes — along with the South African poet Thomas Pringle and others — and that it was she who wrote out the work that was published as the slave narrative of Mary Prince.) In the Caribbean especially, coming to terms with — and freeing oneself from — the slave past, *in the former master's language,* presented a psychic as well as a rhetorical challenge.

I have written elsewhere about Rudyard Kipling's familiar imperialist poem "The White Man's Burden," about how it was composed in 1899 to encourage the USA to prove its worth on the world stage by invading the Philippines and acquiring an Empire of its own, and about how it blatantly demonstrates imperial presumptions about race and monstrosity: "In a language that now jars, the poem blithely assumes that European intervention was a . . . *duty,* and also that the 'heavy harness' of colonial rule would serve a 'fluttered folk and wild — / Your new-caught, sullen peoples, / Half devil and half child.'"[23] By infantilizing the Third World in this way, the imperialist grants himself (in his own eyes at least) the moral justification to rule it. To a twenty-first century reader, there are obvious problems with the assumptions themselves; these problems are exacerbated, however, if the assumptions ever become normalized within the colonies that have been so claimed, and within the minds of those who have then been educated to think of themselves as colonized.

One of the most effective and outspoken opponents of such a mindset, during the later twentieth century, was the Barbadian writer George Lamming. Writing in 1983, about Barbados in 1950, he observes:

> Today I shudder to think how [Britain] . . . could have achieved the miracle of being called Mother. It had made us pupils to its language and its institutions, baptized us in the

same religion; schooled boys in the same game of cricket with its elaborate and meticulous etiquette of rivalry. Empire was not a very dirty word [then], and seemed to bear little relation to those forms of domination we now call imperialist.[24]

Yet another of Lamming's responses was, in its broadest form, parody, as when (in *Water with Berries*) he rewrote Shakespeare's *The Tempest* to foreground Caliban. In parallel fashion, other "Commonwealth" writers have rewritten Daniel Defoe's *Robinson Crusoe* (Derek Walcott's "The Castaway," J.M. Coetzee's *Foe*), Charlotte Brontë's *Jane Eyre* (Jean Rhys's *Wide Sargasso Sea*), Joseph Conrad's *Heart of Darkness* (essays by V.S. Naipaul and Chinua Achebe), and Charles Dickens's *Great Expectations* (Peter Carey's *Jack Maggs*). They have produced these revisionary histories in order to testify to alternative scales of social value. Such parodies were designed not with ridicule — mere dismissal — in mind, but with the tensions between the inherited template and the alternatives embodied in perception and desire: in other words, with *irony* in mind, and its capacity to affirm as both valid and viable a life lived, in the world and in language, at a tangent to that which merely reinscribes the past or reconfirms the status quo.

—୧ V. About Ridicule and Recognition

There are at least two huge categories of irony: that which condescends from a position of presumed power, and that which refuses and seeks to undermine the validity of this first configuration. The one form condescends to that which it sees as exotic or quaint, especially when the observer in this circumstance fails to imagine that anyone *of quality* might think otherwise. For all that Susanna Moodie, for example, in *Roughing It in the Bush,* praises the sublimity and picturesqueness of the scenery, on arriving in Canada, she at the same time declares she is "not a little amused at the extravagant expectations entertained by some of our steerage passengers."[25] These "others" are Irish. Mr. Moodie dismisses them as "savages" (31) and Mrs. Moodie ridicules them (along with the Scots and the regional English) by means of a caricaturing dialect. It would be easy in turn to ridicule *these* presumptions. But it's important to understand that the Moodies class themselves above these "others" partly because the social system in place permits them this luxury: it is as forcefully symbolic as it is documentary when Susanna Moodie records that *others* must go through a "general order of purification" on arrival, but that she and her husband, being "cabin passengers," "were only obliged to send our servant" on shore, with bedding to be washed clean (24).

A gesture of recognition, then, does not necessarily free an observer from the imperial context that has induced it. This dilemma lies at the heart of Sara Jeannette Duncan's 1893 novel *The Simple Adventures of a Memsahib*,[26] where a young woman, who marries into Raj society and observes it with distancing amusement, finds herself against her good intentions becoming part of the class she has ridiculed — because for many competing reasons she cannot belong to anything else. Individuality does not seem to be an option. That was the 1890s. Such imperialism is not limited to the nineteenth century. In one scene in Bharati Mukherjee's *Jasmine*,[27] for example, an American speaks a few words of Vietnamese to a young Vietnamese adoptee in Middle America; instead of showing the relaxed pleasurable response the man anticipates, the boy freezes — for *he knows, knows,* the military circumstances in which this American will have learned these words. In the boy's mind, when the man speaks recognition, he also speaks invasion.

The alternative dimension of irony, that which undermines, emerges in the voices that speak back against imperial preoccupations, even if they sometimes do so covertly. During the years of slavery in the Caribbean, for example, the overseers never managed to control the survival tactics of folktales, especially when the tale-tellers adapted the West African trickster tales of Anansi the spider to local circumstances. In African narrative, Anansi often lost when he embarked on his grand schemes; in the Caribbean, Annancy the black spider always triumphed over the white cockroach. And the plantation managers either didn't understand the message or didn't think it important to understand. Or both. More overt were the political tactics of Australian aboriginal groups in 1988 at the time of the national bicentennial cele-brations of the arrival of the British First Fleet at Botany Bay. One group made a short film called "Babacueria"; another group went to England, planted a flag on the white cliffs of Dover, claimed the land in the name of the Aboriginal peo-ples and allowed that, as a gesture of accommodation, they would permit the natives to continue to live there. In the film — which is itself a kind of parody of such explanation tales as "how the kangaroo got its name" — a number of elaborately uniformed Murri (or Black Australians) row ashore onto the coast of Queensland just where a number of scantily clad white folks are cooking over an open fire. "I say," say the behatted sailors, "what do you call this place?" "Aw yair," say the white folks, with expansive gestures that might or might not be taken as signs of welcome, "we call it a babacueria." As might be expected, this *parodic* edge of irony — which names an entire continent, as it were, for a single "barbecue area" — resolves some issues without directly or even necessarily addressing others. The reality of poverty, for example. Sub-stance abuse, on or off reserves. Urban isolation and early demise. For these, irony is no solution at all, though it might well be a weapon in an arsenal of change.

VI. About Names, Anecdotes, and Alienation

Let me interrupt these comments for a moment to say a bit more about names, including my own. So far as I can find out, my surname is either French in origin — *Le Nève*, the newcomer, the immigrant — or it's an adaptation out of Welsh: *Attanewe*, by the yew tree, in other words the gravedigger. Either way, it positions its wearer on a kind of margin, or boundary zone, between more conventional received identities. But does it mean what it says, and if so, what does that imply? A boundary zone, of course, is a place in its own right, which is another feature of postcolonial ironies. But the word "margin" can mean different things. It applies in one way inside a settlement culture, in another to minority status within any culture, and in a still more general way to the metaphysics of being alive.

To the immigrant settler, a new life simultaneously represents opportunity (a claim on some fresh alternative) and a heart-wrenching separation from all things familiar, leading to psychic and perhaps other more concrete claims upon the old home and tradition. In Margaret Atwood's metaphor, in her poem "Migration: C.P.R.," those emigrants who took the railway west, "wanting / a place of absolute / unformed begin-

47

Ill. 5: Len Peterson's cartoon satirizes Canadian officials' habit of changing the English-language words of the national anthem, "O Canada," and people's consequent uncertainty about which words to sing; at the same time, the cartoon celebrates the nation and its continuing survival. Reprinted from the Vancouver Sun, *and reproduced courtesy of Len Peterson.*

ning,"[28] ended up finding "more secondhand stores" (28) than they expected, and before much time has passed they begin unpacking from luggage they didn't even know they had brought along. I used to read this conclusion as a failure of nerve or desire, but I see it now to function more effectively as a sign of the uncertainty of change as well as of the inevitability of transformation. Not *either/or* but *both/and:* the rhetoric of chaos *rather than but sometimes including* arbitrary neatness, of interconnection *rather than but sometimes including* resistance. (See Ill. 5)

Yet the "both/and" position is not unrelated to perceived power, for the irony of indeterminacy — or at least indeterminacy as far as conventional categories of social order are concerned — takes a somewhat different form in the lives of those whose identities are shaped by two or more (often biracial) heritages. Sometimes these contacts produced dilemmas, as in Robert Sullivan's "Tai Tokerau" poems,[29] which autobiographically take the narrator (of mixed Irish-Maori heritage) into the unfamiliarity of the Maori language and the Maori half of his family; the more he understands, the more the reader must learn Maori also, for the poem increasingly uses, and refuses to translate, Maori words; and the more the narrator knows, the more he understands that the words his family at least initially use with him are those not used for family but kept for strangers. He (and the reader with him) must learn his way across a border, knowing — yet still learning — his way home.

Sometimes, too, cross-cultural contacts have constructed identifiable (if not always recognized) social groups (the *Métis,* for example), and, sometimes these contacts have shaped language as well — as with Michif among the Métis. Even more frequently, however, bicultural contacts in social history have led to dismissive, hurtful, racist comments about the unproductiveness of any mix, which is the basis for numerous realist fictions about social experience (both "Commonwealth" and other).[30] More angrily, the St. Lucian poet Derek Walcott, in a much quoted passage about his own mixed heritage, written early in his career, condemns both European imperialism and Mau-Mau tribal violence, and then asks:

> I who am poisoned with the blood of both,
> Where shall I turn, divided to the vein?
> I who have cursed
> The drunken officer of British rule, how choose
> Between this Africa and the English tongue I love?
> Betray them both, or give back what they give?
> How can I face such slaughter and be cool?
> How can I turn from Africa and live?[31]

An "either/or" choice, in other words, would be self-destructive.

Other examples show yet more social configurations of race and identity — such as the politics of apartheid and the refusal of apartheid, whether in the racial categories once in use in South Africa or in the plantation language of the Caribbean. It is well known that official South African discourse in the twentieth century long insisted on racial segregation. Less appreciated, perhaps, is the way plantation language in Trinidad, Guyana, and Jamaica accepted racial mix as a given, but then used this fact manipulatively to insist on differentiation. The sales value of slaves in the Caribbean relied, that is, on a fine discrimination of complexion; and the plantations regularly used such terms as *zambo* (reinscribed in "Little Black Sambo"), *mulatto, octoroon,* and so on to signify monetary worth. Writers V.S. Naipaul and Edgar Mittelholzer, in such works as "The Baker's Story" and *A*

Morning at the Office,[32] have even observed that a politics of discriminatory behaviour, based on complexion, continued to exist within their society long after slavery had been officially abolished. But plantation language itself has gradually given way. In Trinidad, the powerful mimicry of calypso and carnival contributed to this process of change. Folk performances, such as those of Louise Bennett, functioned like street theatre to countenance and then counsel reform. And after their political independence in 1962, Jamaicans began to refuse the word "dialect" and to refer to their vocabulary and speech sound with the term "nation language." Rastafarian usage, as in the work of Edward Brathwaite, even refused the objective case: it became politically important not to "write me" but "to write I." In both the Caribbean and Africa, moreover, the arbitrariness of using racial categories as systems of personal identification was made ludicrous by irony.

I can clarify one of these situations by rehearsing some statistics as they were reported in the Johannesburg *Star* on March 21, 1986: the statistics establish first of all that people were classified by colour within the existing political system, but also demonstrate that individuals could and did apply to the bureaucratic "authorities" to have their colour category changed, so that in 1985, more than 1000 people officially "changed colour" and were reported by the paper as "chameleons":

- 702 coloured people turned white;
- 19 whites became coloured;
- 1 Indian became white;

- 3 Chinese became white;
- 50 Indians became coloured;
- 43 coloured became Indians;
- 21 Indians became Malay;
- 30 Malays became Indian;
- 249 blacks became coloured;
- 20 coloureds became black;
- 2 blacks became "other Asians";
- 1 black became Griqua;
- 11 coloureds became Chinese;
- 3 coloureds became Malay;
- 1 Chinese became coloured;
- 8 Malays became coloured;
- 3 blacks became Malay; but
- no blacks became white, and
- no whites became black.

Such social realities became the stuff of protest in journalism and politics, the stuff of allegory in much-censored fiction, and the stuff of parody in street theatre and revues.

Ridicule is also the strategy that the Nigerian writer Wole Soyinka uses to unmask and undermine racism in his poem "Telephone Conversation," about a black man seeking a room in a white landlady's London. He "hates a wasted journey," he tells her on the phone, and announces "I am African." But he is unprepared for her response: "how dark?" When she varies the emphasis — "Considerate she was," says the speaker — and asks "are you dark? or very light?" he says "You mean — like plain or milk chocolate?" and tries "West African sepia." But when she says "don't know what that is," he proceeds to expose her racism further by ending his conversation in blank verse:

> 'Facially, I am brunette, but madam, you should see
> The rest of me. Palm of my hand, soles of my feet
> Are a peroxide blonde. Friction, caused —
> Foolishly, madam — by sitting down, has turned
> My bottom raven black — One moment, madam' — sensing
> Her receiver rearing on the thunderclap
> About my ears — 'Madam,' I pleaded, 'wouldn't you rather
> See for yourself?'[33]

Yet, while the poem is a sharp *rhetorical* achievement, it cannot by itself end the reality of discriminatory landlord-and-tenant laws. Moreover, anything like simple in-your-face laughter — most effective when it expresses a firmly-planted self-esteem, as in Soyinka's poem — is seen by other writers as an inadequate gesture when self-denigration is the likelier experience of and in the world. But this distinction does not mean that irony disappears. For example, self-denigration is the state of mind in which Edward Brathwaite's great quest poem, *The Arrivants,* begins; the opening section "Rights of Passage" spells out the swirl of unacceptable identities that the former slaves of the Caribbean had to live with for much of the twentieth century. Ironic voices *present* these identities. But Brathwaite closes his poem neither by tolerating the racist language that exists in the present nor by suggesting that history is easy to revise or the past easy to reclaim. West Indians who pretend to reidentify with an integrity they imagine in the African past, Brathwaite suggests, are fooling themselves. He affirms instead the vitality of a people *in* the Caribbean *in* the present, mixed and free, who realize that they are not constrained by Empire but capable of

> making
> with their
>
> rhythms some-
> thing torn
>
> and new[34]

The syncopation that resonates in vernacular Bajan speech also adapts here the edge of intrinsically violent protest that characterizes the Petro rites of Vodun, those *"plus raide"*[35] rites that developed in the Caribbean: disruptive but creative, disruptive *in order to be* creative: violence and speech.

But who is the *eiron* here, if one exists at all? the one who, by conventional definitions of *irony*,[36] cannot speak directly, can speak but won't be heard, can speak but is heard only within a context that understands tone, doesn't believe in speaking, doesn't believe in a world of order, doesn't believe in the listener-receiver's world of order, doesn't believe he or she as a speaker has the ability to speak in or be in or speak to that world of order, or who believes in the world of order but cannot connect it with a belief in the self? The *eiron*. The vocabulary circling through this list raises even more questions, of course — about the validity of "order" or a "world of order" in the first place, or perhaps most of all the usefulness of even speaking.[37]

An answer of sorts to these questions, however, can be seen in a poem by the Malaysian-born Australian poet Ee

Tiang Hong; it's called "Coming To," and the irony of Ee's title will be obvious. It's conveyed by pun, by what ironists call "oversetting," the deliberate play of double-hearing. At one level the poem tells of being in an automobile accident (on a bridge), briefly knocked unconscious and likely overturned (for the car ends up in water), and (shortly after) regaining a sense of being alive and being in place. It begins:

> It was a blind corner,
> I remember, I couldn't think
> to brake somehow, still less in time,
> That moment round the bend —
> a shock of water, overwhelming sea
> where should have been a road,
> a bridge over the river,
> I mean even in flood.

After a "sensation of floating," the narrator (who likely has come from "overseas") somehow regains *"terra firma, Australis,"* and opens his eyes to see "new faces, fellow Australian."

> And a country woman asking:
> 'Where y' from?'
> Her husband stands up tall
> by their four-wheel drive,
> looks me up and down:
> (Jesus! What on earth!)
> And so uncertain, 'Perth',
> I said, from down under.[38]

Clearly, the poem is more than a simple personal anecdote, and more complex, for it's also about being both an immigrant and a traveller, moving through culture as well as through space and consciousness — "coming *to*." It could also

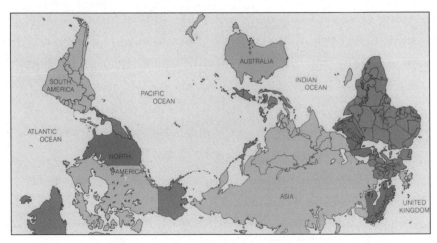

Ill. 6: This reverse of conventional representations of world cartography plays with the politics of the phrase "down under." It appears throughout Australia and New Zealand on maps, postcards, and T-shirts, variously affirming that New Zealand is "no longer down under," or that Australia is "on top" or "up over."

be a poem that simply balances exclusion with exclusivity, of being the ordinary *eiron* who cannot speak; but Ee does more. He reclaims to his own purposes the characteristic vocabulary of Othering (*blind corner, round the bend, bridge, Terra Australis, Where y' from,* 'up over' *down under*) that in "ordinary" Australian discourse would exclude him. In other words, he uses the voice, the strategies of oral ironic narrative, to counter the distancing resonance of *alienation* (see Ill. 6).

—⌒ VII. About Home, and Voice, and
Finding Home Again

When my father completed the eighth grade, my grand-
father required him to quit school and get a job. I have never
been sure if this directive was an impatient response to aca-
demic performance, or a sign of the economic times in East
Vancouver, or a late Victorian presumption about codes of
masculinity. Or all of the above. My father never said. A prac-
tical man, my father ultimately became a vehicle mechanic, a
man adept at reading the logic of machines, but that was
after a couple of forays along other paths — one into the new-
fangled world of electricity, an apprenticeship he actively dis-
liked, and one into the merchant marine. A lover of the sea,
he embarked in his early teens as a deckhand aboard one of
the last motor-assisted sailing vessels to be built in North
Vancouver, the *Geraldine Wolven*. The ship, I assume now, was
named for a person. For years I thought the name was the
Geraldine Wolverine, and fashioned for the boat and its crew a
thousand tales of wilderness adventure on the high seas.
Once again the real story was more ordinary: a cargo of lum-
ber was taken to Sydney, Australia; a cargo of coal was taken
to, yes, Newcastle, New South Wales; then the next scheduled

voyage, which would have taken the crew to Hong Kong, was cancelled when the First World War made Pacific crossings dangerous — and indeed the *Geraldine Wolven* did play games of hide-and-seek with German warships off the coast of Fiji in the unelectrified dark. The ship was on its way back to Canada by this time, and when it reached home port, my father signed out. So much for adventure. Tales of derring-do did not become the stock-in-trade of my childhood bedtime. But my father *was* a wonderful story-*reader,* and in due course Oz and the Emerald City came alive in his *voice.* But that was then, when Oz existed only in fantasy and on the page. Later, in another context, I discovered the Australian penchant for abbreviation that repositioned "Oz" for real in the South Pacific — and I learned, too, how voice and linguistic playfulness, across several generations, helped transform the South Pacific from a place that Australians called exile into a place they called home.[39] I also came to realize that the quest for home — one of the most recurrent motifs in nineteenth- and twentieth-century postcolonial writing — means a number of different things: the wish to claim new territory and try to feel comfortable in it, and to reclaim old territory or one's power within it, to redetermine the hierarchies of power that shape conventions and "norms" within a given space, and to ruffle the boundary lines that establish hierarchies in the first place.

To recapitulate, then, irony is a way of finding an alternative to the simple oppositional and reinscriptive strategies of critical and literary composition, both of which retain, even in refusing its significance, some version of imperial *centrali-*

ty. Empires — declarations of global norm — do that to you: constructing their own importance, and then buttressing this version of "normality" or "reality" — or "home" (perhaps another word for "comfortable ideology") — by means of military might, sectarian fervour, economic suasion, botanical transplant, architectural nostalgia, and hierarchies of linguistic propriety. Patriarchally, they insist that their colonies are "primitive,"[40] therefore that they require the Empire's "guidance" (for which read *rule*), and affirm, too, that the language of a *colonial* culture is etymologically that of the *farmer* and by definition rough, rude, childlike, and uncultivated. The alternative family tree model of Mother Country and Her Children is not unrelated and not accidental in its design: it reaffirms as virtuous a kind of "protective" political authority at the same time as it tropes the colony as inconsequential. Irony proves to be a pungent way of writing back.

And here's where the Empire's grandchildren come in. Not unrelated to what has gone before, they speak — or *can* speak — obliquely, with a purpose. For while irony *appears* to be using the common words of Empire, it twists them so that the speaker can construct a separate political space within the loosely shared language. It demands that the *listener* adapt to the speaker's *voice,* not simply receive "as given" the speaker's *words* — or else hear nothing, and miss the speaker's point entirely. The consequences of *not hearing* are, of course, many. An insensitive listener can assume that the speaker has *said* nothing, and if the listener is the real power-holder in this transaction he or she will continue to dismiss and diminish the margin-dweller; a more positive listener can tune in to

the obliquity if not the message, and begin to suspect alternative perspectives; and a passive listener can just be set aside,
made irrelevant by failing to appreciate that power will slip
over time from one version of centre to another, travel with
inventiveness and skill and not rest with imitation. The active
listener, by contrast, the one who *hears*, will learn that sharing
a tonality as well as a vocabulary provides an opportunity to
recognize how power-in-language moves.

Hence yet another group of writers ironized the power
structure of Empire in order to free themselves — and their
language — into possibility. A few examples will illustrate.
First, parody, with innuendo. V.S. Naipaul's short story "B.
Wordsworth" begins by declaring that "B." is for "Black,"
there already being a "W." (or "White") Wordsworth, who
may be a poet but can't translate to the Caribbean with any
ease or efficacy. Second, critique, with stiletto. Austin Clarke
titles his autobiography *Growing Up Stupid Under the Union
Jack*, meaning that he was educated to understand Elsewhere
but not "here," the place where he lived.[41] Third, comic
burlesque, with recuperative intent, as in a well-known Australian folksong "Botany Bay," which deals with the transportation of convicts out of England; while its jauntiness
scarcely represents the violence of the times, it nevertheless
conveys with admirable clarity some particular social consequences: Australia's characteristic (perhaps stereotypical)
refusal to accept the law of the times as fair, for example, or
the language of received social status as uncontestable. One
stanza of the song declares the speaker's condition:

> 'Tain't leaving old England we cares about,
> 'Tain't cos we misspells wot we knows,
> But because all we light-fingered gentry
> Hops round with a log on our toes.

Shackled, that is. The final stanza issues a countervailing moral, with advice to those who think themselves the convicts' "betters":

> Now, all my young Dook-ies and Duch-ess-es,
> Take warning from what I've to say —
> Mind all is your own as you touch-es-es,
> Or you'll meet us in Botany Bay.[42]

But a simple refusal of linguistic rules does not necessarily deconstruct them, whether in "Botany Bay" (where syntax and phonology are disrupted but not standard sentence order) or in Louky Bersianik's *L'Eugélionne*,[43] where an interplanetary visitor to Québec exposes the gendered hierarchies of French grammar but cannot instantly change them. A much more common strategy is to reclaim the vernacular — any vernacular — from the dismissive category of regional or class "dialect" and to reinvest local speech sound with the power of political revelation, as in much of Edward Brathwaite or Derek Walcott in the Caribbean, or Frank Moorehouse and Bruce Dawe in Australia.[44]

A fourth example of ironic exposé will illustrate one of the ways in which this vernacular technique works; it comes from the Singapore writer Arthur Yap, whose poem "a lesson on the definite article" at once satirizes a fellow-citizen for aping foreign models of behaviour and expatiates on a variety of uses of that feature of the English language that is particularly difficult for second-language learners: the article, *the,* and its many applications. The poem pointedly, however, avoids the use of "the" until halfway through. It reveals what a narrator hears when he eavesdrops on a "bearded man" and a "girl with bank-teller's eyes" at the next table in a crowded restaurant. Conversations here are only half heard; speech at one table is "graded" into others' ears — *graded:* both recorded on a gradient and re-*marked* on. And the unidentified narrator hears a bearded (English?) man say:

> I really love chinese food, you people can cook
> beautifully, the bearded man had also a large appetite.
> I can't cook, & her non-sequitur
> 'the poor chinese are like the 2nd class jews'
> provoked these possibilities:
> poor chinese are like 2nd class jews,
> poor chinese are like the 2nd class jews,
> the poor chinese are like 2nd class jews.

The narrator then assesses what the conversation has told him:

> the she was, by the way, the chinese
> & her the accent, showing she had arrived,
> gone the places, reached the it,
> made the it, confirmed she was the.[45]

The poem sets out a kind of grammar of declining, of competitive neocolonialisms and the power of observant, ironic detachment from them. The set of semantic variations, moreover, spells out trenchantly the distance between the "definite article" and the "genuine article," the power to identify and the worth of identity.

Other examples multiply: Allen Curnow's "House and Land" where, even with several voices available to them, the citizens of the new New Zealand still cannot feel at home; or Louise Bennett's performance poetry, opining at one point that England might have some difficulty undergoing "colonizin' in reverse"; or Zulfikar Ghose's "The Remove," where a London classroom proves to be a site where Sikh and Muslim children meet to learn English while their families back home "periodically accuse each other of aggression."[46] Ghose's poem reads in part:

> The Sikh from Ambala in East Punjab,
> India, formerly in the British Empire,
> the Muslim from Sialkot in West Punjab,
> Pakistan, formerly British India,
> the Sikh boy and the Muslim boy are two
> of twenty such Sikhs and Muslims
> from East Punjab and West Punjab, which
> formerly were the Punjab,
> standing together in assembly, fearfully
> miming the words of a Christian hymn.

Their teacher, Mr Iqbal — "which can be a Sikh name or a Muslim name, / *Mohammed* Iqbal or Iqbal *Singh* . . . / comes from Jullundur in East Punjab / but near enough to the border to be almost / West Punjab" — shouts at them to be quiet.

> And so: twenty years after
> the Union Jack came down on Delhi
> and the Punjab became East Punjab and
> West Punjab and the Sikhs did not like it
> and the Muslims did not like the Sikhs
> not liking it and they killed each other
> not by the hundred nor by the thousand

but by the hundred thousand, here then
is Mr Iqbal with his remove class of
twenty Punjabis, some Sikh and some Muslim,
in a Secondary Modern School in London,
all of them trying to learn English."[47]

The politics of rivalry takes a particularly biting form here, in a rhetoric of class and cumulative negation. The poem builds from mere impatience — or what takes on the features of impatience — to social and historical castigation, underlining the power — and the inadequacy — of "Remove." Diasporic exile, isolation, categorical enclosure. Here, as elsewhere, moreover, the politics lies in the voice.

To place Eli Mandel's poem "First Political Speech" beside Ghose's critique of "ESL" containment is to see that even what looks like a more cavalier *found poem* is by no means innocent of judgment. At first glance Mandel's verse might seem like mere banter, but closer attention to its *voice* reveals that the poet's apparently arbitrary arrangement of a list of fifty "transition words" from a composition textbook is deliberately designed. When given its new, decontextualizing, relocating title, "First Political Speech," it turns into a devastating exposé of the emptiness of bureaucratic bafflegab, the kind that often sustains and directs the status quo. The poem begins:

first, in the first place, to begin with, secondly,
in the second place, lastly

Drifting cumulatively through "again, also, . . . furthermore, . . . besides, [and] similarly," it reaches "for instance, another" without ever specifying anything. Then instantly it qualifies — "nevertheless, still, however, at the same time" — ignores logic to assert "certainly, surely, doubtless, indeed, perhaps, possibly, / probably, anyway, in all probability," leaps to "therefore," and closes with flamboyant and unfounded assurance:

> the foregoing, the preceding, as previously mentioned
>
> as already stated[48]

From these examples, a *reader* might well believe that the institutions of authority, simply by doing nothing, will continue forever unchanged, or else erase identity by hiding behind the ordered facelessness called "globalism." But irony repeatedly exposes these institutions' inadequacies, if one is willing to *listen;* and implicitly, if not openly, the irony countenances — and reaches towards — reform.

—ᔕ VIII. About Learning to Read
and Learning to Hear

In the summers, when I was small, my father grew vegetables in the back garden, directed traceries of scarlet runner beans along the lane fence, planted carrots and potatoes to store against the winter, burying them deep below a literal frost line, as insurance — in case the frost was figurative as well. My father also tried to teach me directly many things: to play tennis, swim, repair the Model A Ford, and row against the current. Generations do learn from each other's authority, of course — but not always directly. Sometimes they go off on tangents, choose to differ rather then simply repeat. In my own case, over the course of time, I learned to play squash, plant potatoes, read rocks, and repair sentences. Some neighbours asked when I was going to quit school and get a job, and then later on asked when I was going to quit what I was doing and get a *real* job. My father refused to repeat *his* history; I would go to school as long as I wanted to, as long as it was worth doing, and if I could. Neither of us imagined the extent of the commonwealth of learning.

I am reminded of R.K. Narayan, recalling how he learned English in India from "the best teacher in the school, if not by the ruling star of the institution, the headmaster himself" — but that the English primer, however sturdily bound, was less than immediately comprehensible. It began "'A was an Apple Pie' (see Ill. 7) . . . and went on to explain, 'B bit it' and 'C cut it'. The activities of B and C were understandable [Narayan writes], but the opening line itself was mystifying. . . .

Ill. 7: Kate Greenaway's A Apple Pie (1886) was one of the most popular alphabet books of its day. It quickly became a classic of children's literature, and a model for the teaching of reading both in England and "abroad." The culturally specific illustrations and references suggest why Narayan's classmates would be puzzled.

From B's and C's zestful application, we could guess that it had to do with . . . eating. But what was it that was being eaten?" When the "omniscient one, our English teacher" could not answer this question, Narayan recalls that "We were left free to guess, each according to his capacity, at the quality, shape, and details, of the civilization portrayed in our class books."[49]

But I am reminded, too, of Chinua Achebe, wondering

why his Nigerian schoolmates should have been ashamed of their past, choosing kerosene tins over waterpots so as to look contemporary, saying "winter" instead of "harmattan" in order not to be laughed at. "I remember the shock," Achebe writes, "felt by Christians of my father's generation in my village in the early 'forties when for the first time the local girls' school performed Nigerian dances at the anniversary of the coming of the gospel. Hitherto they had always put on something Christian and civilized which I think was called the Maypole dance." Such observations, he adds, provided "an adequate revolution for me to espouse — to help my society regain its belief in itself and put away the complexes of the years of denigration and self-denigration." Affirming what he takes to be his great responsibility as a novelist, he declares that his intention is to "teach my readers that their past — with all its imperfections — was not one long night of savagery from which the first Europeans acting on God's behalf delivered them."[50]

But consider also how the more-than-generational shift between nation-language and "standard" English reinforces a political point in "Yuh Hear 'Bout?" by Jamaican-born Valerie Bloom, now an English resident. It begins with a question::

> Yuh hear bout di people dem arres
> Fi bun dung di Asian people dem house?

Other examples follow, in a continuing series of questions: how about "di policeman dem lock up / Fi beat up di black bwoy widout a cause?" or "di MP dem sack because im refuse fi help / im coloured constituents in a dem fight 'gainst deportation?" No-one has heard, says the poem, letting this conclusion resonate — briefly — for the poem then repeats the questions in a so-called "standard" register, still seeking a listener:

> Did you hear about the people they arrested
> For burning down the Asian people's house?

Or about "the policeman they put in jail / For beating up the black boy without any cause?" Or "the MP they sacked / because he refused to help / his black constituents in their fight / against deportation?" With no more positive an answer forthcoming when the questions are asked in this form, the poem then cryptically closes:

> You didn't hear about them?
> Me neither.[51]

The point is not only Who Hears the message in the two forms of discourse, but also Who Listens: who *bothers* to listen. What is "standard" and what is not, and who has the power to say? As John Agard comments in "Listen Mr Oxford don,"

> I en serving no jail sentence
> I slashing suffix in self-defence
> I bashing future wit present tense
> and if necessary
>
> I making de Queen's English accessory
> to my offence[52]

In many ways, Patrick White's extraordinary novel *A Fringe of Leaves* (1976) encapsulates many of the issues that irony — as I have been talking *about* it — addresses: social history, class and marginality, uncertainty, order, adaptation —

and it applies many of the compositional strategies that I have been alluding to: tonal management, silence, indirection, reclaimed metaphor, and double-hearing. The novel is loosely based on the wreck of the *Sterling Castle* off the coast of Australia in 1836, and on the real-life narrative of captivity, performance, and madness that followed — in other words, the subsequent history of one of the ship's surviving passengers, a woman named Eliza Fraser, who in real life went on to be a kind of travelling raconteur, telling her story as a cautionary moral fable about civilization and savagery to whoever would pay.[53]

In White's novel, the characters serve a somewhat different function from that of the captivity tale. Most obviously, the novel tells of a Cornishwoman, Ellen Gluyas, who marries up in society, is trained by her mother-in-law, Mrs. Roxburgh, to lose her local accent, and to acquire society manners and approvable taste. Ellen then accompanies her husband Austin to Australia, to visit his brother Garnet. In a characteristic White gesture, the brothers are complementary, Austin being the conservative, Garnet the radical who has been sent to Australia to distance him from Received Behaviour. After Ellen and Garnet have a brief but passionate fling, she and Austin begin to return north, with the intention of sailing home. The word "Garnet" comes etymologically from the same root as "pomegranate," which makes explicit White's narrative strategy: he is rewriting the Persephone story here in the down-underworld of Van Diemen's Land, but in this instance, the circle back to spring will be long delayed.

For after stopping briefly in Sydney, the Roxburghs' ship

is wrecked on a reef, the crew struggle free from the hierarchical restrictions of shipboard only to meet other, more
immediate, deaths; Austin (more concerned with saving his
copy of Virgil's *Georgics* than with facing reality) is quickly
dispatched by a Murri spear, and Ellen is taken captive to
become a nursemaid to aboriginal children. The novel then
details Ellen's life in the bush, her return to her Cornish
tongue, her encounter with an escaped convict, her second
"landing" in civilization, and her slow and ambivalent accommodation to the fact that what she has learned about life
does not change the world in which she lives; it changes only
her capacity to accept her mental and emotional distance
from received order. While she once perceived her "difference" as a character flaw — because it was cast as a social dis-
grace — by the end of the part of her story that White tells,
she comes elliptically to terms with her separation. She knows
that her newly acquired depth of understanding will not permit her to live happily, in concord; she will, however, be able
to live inside society's apparent institutions but outside their
codified values. The irony of her recognition may, I suppose,
be read as some version of existential despair; yet from
another perspective, irony is the only source of strength that
permits her to go on.

At the same time, the novel is telling another, perhaps
more covert narrative. It makes clear that most of the male
characters whose lives touch Ellen's can never actually see
who she is or hear the story that her experience tells. They
live inside the institutions they inherit or design, accept their
order as real, mistake surfaces for depth, artifice for social

policy, their own limited perceptions for understanding, and they confuse privilege and opportunity with nature and natural right. This litany of confusions might in some literary hands turn into simple loud diatribe; White conveys it — likely aware of the metatextual irony here — through artifice. He wrings polemic out of metaphor, out of voice and oblique exchange: a combination of the political and the sonic.

Listen to how the novel begins, at the Circular Quay, the dock in Sydney, where the Roxburghs' ship has briefly stopped on its way back home — as though nothing had happened in the turbulent south, though the characters are already conflicted. The three characters who speak are just leaving the wharf after having paid a duty call on the Roxburghs (whom they have categorized as visiting gentry). They are Mr. Stafford Merivale and his wife (who have little to do with subsequent narrative actions, though they set out the problem of imperceptiveness here) and Miss Scrimshaw (a woman of no money but upperclass connections whose angular perceptions will ultimately frame and place Ellen Roxburgh's story). And they are the elite of Sydney, or at least consider themselves to be so:

> As the carriage drew away from the Circular Wharf Mr Stafford Merivale tapped the back of his wife's hand and remarked that they had done their duty.
>
> 'No one,' Mrs Merivale replied, 'can accuse me of neglecting duty.' She might have pouted if inherent indolence had not prevailed, and a suspicion that those acquainted with her must know that her claim was not strictly true.
>
> So she smoothed the kid into which her hands had been stuffed, and added, 'At least we were, I think, agreeably entertained. And that is always compensation for any kind of incon-

venience. Miss Scrimshaw,' she asked, looking not quite at her friend, 'weren't we entertained?'

'Oh yes, *most* agreeably,' the latter answered in a rush, which transposed what must have been a deep voice into a higher, unnatural key. 'Living at such a distance nobody can fail to be refreshed by visitors from Home. The pity is when their visits are so brief.'

Mrs Merivale decided to appear satisfied, while Miss Scrimshaw, obviously, was not. An atmosphere of unconfessed presentiment was intensified by the slight creaking of woodwork and friction of leather in the comfortably upholstered carriage. Rocked together and apart by the uneven surface of the street the occupants were at the mercy of the land as seaborne passengers are threatened by the waves.

'Short visits make no demands,' Mrs Merivale consoled herself. 'Don't you agree?' Mr Merivale being a man, there was no question but that her remark was intended for Miss Scrimshaw.

'Oh yes,' she answered as expected, 'there is that about short visits.'

In all the large circle of her acquaintance it was Miss Scrimshaw's duty to agree, which was why her voice sounded only on some occasions her own. In exceptional circumstances, however, she would express an opinion, and it was this, together with her strong nose, long teeth, and Exalted Connection, which caused the Mrs Merivales of Sydney to glance not quite at their companion and hope they were accepted.

'Who can guess,' Mrs Merivale ventured to pursue the subject, 'from exchanging a few friendly words, with strangers, on a ship's deck, what demands a longer visit might entail.'

At that point the carriage lurched.

'Oh no, people can be frightful!' Miss Scrimshaw asserted, rather flat, but surprisingly loud. 'I do not believe one will ever arrive at the end of people's frightfulness.'

This was an exceptional circumstance, and it made Mrs Merivale quail inside her fur palatine.

'I don't know,' her husband began, who had been content until now to leave it to the ladies, and to sit staring in transparent pleasure at whatever object presented itself the other side of the carriage window; 'I don't believe I've ever come across a fellow in whom I didn't find a fair measure of good.'

There was so much that his sex and nature must always prevent him understanding, the two ladies were at once reduced to a collusive silence.[54]

Consider how White establishes at the outset the inadequate voice of institutional authority. Merivale does not touch or stroke or hold his wife's hand, he *taps* the *back* of it, a presumptive gesture; these hands of hers, moreover, as though not even part of her, have passively *been stuffed* into kid gloves. Mrs. Merivale's sense of her real position in relation to authority apparently even affects her speech. For asserting that she at least has been *agreeably entertained,* she tempers her enthusiasm by speaking in the same breath of *inconvenience.* But of course neither she nor Miss Scrimshaw appears to feel that they *can* communicate — directly — anything real. For her part, until she permits *one* to speak *surprisingly loudly* of *frightfulness,* Miss Scrimshaw evasively just echoes Mrs. Merivale, acting the reflective counsellor, permitting the anxious counsel-seeker to continue speaking. White's careful negatives spell out this anxiety, clearly if not openly: Mrs. Merivale is aware that her claim is *not strictly true,* she looks *not quite at her friend,* she asks *Don't you agree?* in order to confirm what she thinks she ought to find true.

Already a social hierarchy is in place — not just the one that positions all these characters near the top, along with the Roxburghs offstage, the Exalted Connection, and Home — but also the entire implied social system of ruler and ruled: the civil, religious, and military authorities on the one hand, and on the other those who have been *transported* and *trans-*

posed. All of them, certainly the three characters aboard the coach, are *rocking,* threatened somehow by the sea that divides them from the system they have always accepted as the arbiter of normal relations, and by the land, Australia itself, the continent that stretches inland away from them, into the real bush and the imaginary Outback: a territory defined by the institution of their own law as *terra nullius,* but which is nevertheless peopled in their minds by figures they construct as Other, as *animal* and *savage.*

Consider also the covert running metaphor in the first pages of *A Fringe of Leaves:* it's bound up in the words *duty, accuse, suspicion, claim, true, stuffed, compensation, transport, distance, unnatural key, unconfessed presentiment, mercy, threatened, entail, ventured to pursue, arrive at the end, collusive silence.* Embedded in this sequence is a slant picture of the transportation system, the convict history that constitutes a kind of deep grammar of Australian cultural life. But White's further point in this novel is that, characteristically, the men don't hear the inadequacy of their own passivity, their blithe acceptance of *whatever* they see — and whatever they see as the judiciousness of the status quo, the *fair measure of good* they presume at the expense of serious analysis or social reform. Not Stafford Merivale, not Austin Roxburgh, not the villainous second mate Mr. Pilcher or the vapid Reverend Mr. Cottle, not Lieutenant Cunningham, Mr. Oakes, Captain Purdew, or the Commandant. However often and even sincerely these men might seek confirmation in ritual, they are deaf to nuance and blind to what Ellen and Miss Scrimshaw repeatedly, if enigmatically, see. Who, then, is imprisoned?

White's answer, of course, written out in narrative, is that they all are: prisoners of class and gender, space and time, but of their own minds most of all and their resistance to change. Ellen and Miss Scrimshaw at least come equivocally to terms with the disparity between their freedom to see and their confinement by social category. The rest of the characters never question how they themselves perceive, or why — never ask *what if* the systems of rule and behaviour and presumed authority that they accept as "normal" and "natural" are not so.

White does not preach opposition here, though he was something of an irascible social rebel in real life, especially as he aged, and for all the apparent formality of his prose he was a radical stylist as well. It is in the style, moreover — in the *voicing* of alternative ways of understanding, not through anything so direct as moral statement or public action — that he finally elucidates the last of the four epigraphs he appends to *A Fringe of Leaves,* the one from the surrealist-Marxist-French patriot Louis Aragon: "Love is your last chance. There is really nothing else on earth to keep you there." White dramatizes this riddle of human existence as irony: as a circling realization that distance and loss are felt signs of connection, that connection does not efface independence, that to deny connection is to refuse personal power, that personal power comes attached to distance and loss. He also insists that, however pessimistic he might be about the likelihood of human beings behaving with humanity, this ironic circle of existence should give rise neither to simple cynicism nor to paralytic despair.

—ᵒ IX. *About Refusing Definition*

"For Sappho," writes the poet Anne Carson, "irony is a verb. It places her in a certain relation / to her own life. / Silk and bitter. / How very interesting (the woman thinks) to watch myself / construct this. / She is at work / on her essay."[55] Carson's Sappho is in dialogue here with Socrates and dallying with the temptations of ridicule. But neither silk alone nor bitterness alone can be her conclusion. Neither is it Carson's. Nor is it mine. Carson, however, seeks mysticism as irony's tantalizing opposite; I see human affirmation as irony's oblique achievement. I therefore close with a tribute to my first teachers, who gave me the freedom to speak and the freedom to disagree. My parents' quiet wit and shared knowledge — the common wealth of being alive — held me in place even as I looked away (and they encouraged me to look away) into the farther riddling corners of space and metaphor and academe.

When my father retired, he continued to till the back garden, but he began to grow roses for the tabletop instead of winter carrots to bury underground. He also turned to carpentry, and built shelves, and toys, and bookends. He crafted each set of bookends with a particular person in mind, decorating each to appeal to whoever was to receive it. Perched on the lateral flats of one set were hand-carved tugboats; on others were samples of drilling core, painted rocket ships, or moving mechanical wheels. Some even displayed wooden books, with "pages" gilded and "covers" etched to look like leather. One set sat on the fireplace mantel, holding upright and in place each of my own books as they came into print. My father and I did not talk about literature directly. We talked garden lore and the rules of snooker instead, hockey and Hong Kong, India and Oz: in other words, the round earth's imagined corners and the ironic bureaucracies of local truths. Why do I tell you this? Because I am talking *about*. In order to suggest, out of my own experience, how the world of reading and the world of ordinary living interconnect.

The Australian novelist Thea Astley helps here. "Living," she writes, "is serial, an unending accretion of alternatives."[56] It's a textual metaphor, suggesting that each of us, in writing, rereads our life, and each of us, in reading, rewrites it. But the implications go further. I have made clear the limitations of the rhetoric of family in discussing the Commonwealth; if at the same time — like other grandchildren of Empire — I nevertheless (ironically) use it, I do so aware of how the individual voice and the local context can challenge the idea of uniformity and dislocate the simple linear paradigms by which empires (whether political or economic, linguistic or technological, sectarian or familial) claim power and precedence. Honouring another generation, therefore, is not to relive it, but to recognize it, and in so doing to assert the inevitability and the creativity of difference. To celebrate the cumulative "accretion of alternatives," moreover — the difficult voices of pain and discord as well as those of commonality and prospect and joy — is also to recognize the power of irony as an agent of transformation, in the Commonwealth and elsewhere. For the contra-dictory voices of irony are strategies of affirmation. They resist arbitrary assumptions about the approvable shape of the world. They assert the freedom to speak, the need to listen, and the opportunity to be heard.

Ill. 8: A commercial sign outside a Vancouver ironmongery. Does it suggest that one of the ironies of irony is that it has its own rules?

NOTES

1. Toronto: U Toronto P, 1935; 2nd ed. 1948. After reviewing "the meanings and history of irony" in Cicero, Quintilian, Socrates, Aristotle, Goethe, Lucretius, Bacon, Greek drama, and Shakespeare, Sedgewick defines "dramatic irony" as "the sense of an illusion under control of knowledge but beyond control of interference" (114).

2. Commentaries on irony usually stress one or more of the following topics: origins, functions, and applications; verbal techniques; the ethics of irony in practice; and irony as more of a psychosocial perception. Among many books on the subject, two by D.C. Muecke — *Irony* (London: Methuen, 1970) and the more extended *The Compass of Irony* (London: Methuen, 1969) — survey most generally the concept of irony, attempting definitions of the term, and classifications of structures involving duality and incongruity (whether in events, dilemmas, self-betrayals, general human history, or drama); Muecke also reviews the term's function, history, morality, and importance. Like other commentators — among them Charles I. Glicksberg (*The Ironic Vision in Modern Literature*. The Hague: Martinus Nijhoff, 1969), Norman Knox (in his specialized survey, *The Word IRONY and Its Context, 1500-1755*. Durham, NC: Duke UP, 1961), Joseph A. Dane (*The Critical Mythology of Irony*. Athens, GA: U Georgia P, 1991), and D.J. Enright (in the essays collected as *The Alluring Parable*. Oxford: Oxford UP, 1988) — Muecke alludes to irony among classical writers (particularly Sophocles) and then traces several forms of European and American irony in post-Medieval times. Among the writers and subjects these critics severally address are Shakespearian ironies in drama, the vexed term "Romantic irony" (as variously applied in the works of Pascal, Schlegel, Kierkegaard, Hegel, Nietzsche, Tolstoy, and

Hardy), critical irony (as in the critical practice of Cleanth Brooks), paradox, mystification, indirection, and nihilism. Morton Gurewitch (*The Ironic Temper and the Comic Imagination*. Detroit: Wayne State UP, 1994) examines further the relation between the lightness and darkness of ironic humour. Ernst Behler (*Irony and the Discourse of Modernity*. Seattle and London: U Washington P, 1990) and Gary J. Handwerk (*Irony and Ethics in Narrative from Schlegel to Lacan*. New Haven and London: Yale UP, 1985) pursue the ramifications of twentieth-century ironic philosophies (as in the writings of Derrida, Habermas, Beckett, and the strategies of postmodernism), and they question the ethics of irony. Handwerk argues that Beckett's ironies simply reinforce readers' sense of their own ignorance, Behler that postmodernism is self-referential, the paradox being that in both instances subjectivity is lost. Enright also alludes to irony's moral charge — arguing that it asserts "negative freedom" (149), functions by "reverberation" (164), combats censorship, and therefore actively exerts an oppositional voice in a politically repressive regime. Linda Hutcheon (*Irony's Edge*. London and New York: Routledge, 1994), looking at Wagner among other figures, connects emotional with ethical issues, and asks if the politics of appropriateness might also mean the end of irony. Northrop Frye, in *Anatomy of Criticism* (Princeton, NJ: Princeton UP, 1957), treats irony as an entire mode of discourse (one distinct from comedy, tragedy, and romance) rather than as an ethical stance or a rhetorical technique. Wayne C. Booth, in *The Rhetoric of Irony* (Chicago and London: U Chicago P, 1974), treats clashes of style, conflicts of fact, voiced warnings, and metaphor as strategies of identifying irony; Booth also comments further on the problem of the failure to recognize an ironic statement (whether because of ignorance, bias, inattention, or emotional inadequacy). Katharina Barbe, in *Irony in Context* (Amsterdam and Philadelphia: John Benjamins, 1995), taking a cognitive linguistic approach to an analysis of irony's techniques and usages, focuses in part on the function of voice and the role of the hearer (as with the character of a political joke in an oppressive system); she also stresses the importance of "situational knowledge" (150).

3. Lewis Carroll, *The Annotated Alice*. Intro. Martin Gardner. New York: Clarkson N. Potter, 1960: 95.

4. See also Linda Hutcheon, *A Theory of Parody*. New York and

London: Methuen, 1985; esp. 52-68. Hutcheon emphasizes that irony is not limited to its semantic function as *antiphrasis* (or speaking by means of an opposite), but also has an obvious, therefore usually overlooked, pragmatic function: "it judges" (53).

5. "How Poems Work," *Globe and Mail* (25 Aug 2001): D18.

6. "'Commonwealth Literature' Does Not Exist" (1983), in *Imaginary Homelands*. London: Granta and Viking, 1991: 61-70.

7. "Orwell and I," *Toronto Review of Contemporary Writing Abroad* 19.3 (Summer 2001): 15-20.

8. "Cook's Mountains," *Cry Ararat!* Toronto: McClelland and Stewart, 1967: 16.

9. *WLWE* 30.2 (1990): 10-16.

10. In *The Location of Culture* (London & New York: Routledge, 1994) and elsewhere. The subject of "hybridity" is of course much more complex, and in recent years has become the contested subject of theoretical debate, involving such terms as cross-fertilization, contamination, forced pairing, fragmentation, sterility, mimicry, resistance to conformity, transculturalism, and the politics of inequality. For critics who problematize the term, see, eg., Benita Parry, "Problems in current discourse theory," *Oxford Literary R* 9 (1987): 27-58; Robert Young, *Colonial Desire: Hybridity in Theory, Culture and Race*. London: Routledge, 1995; and Shalini Puri, "Canonized Hybridities, Resistance Hybridities," in *Caribbean Romances*, ed. Belinda Edmondson. Charlottesville: UP of Virginia, 1999: 12-38. I am indebted to Laura Moss for this reference.

11. For example, while no amount of duplication ever *justifies* the practice, Asian, African, and Amerindian history makes clear that it was not just Europeans who behaved imperially, occupied others' lands, displaced others' cultures, took slaves: nor are European cultures *by definition* either admirable or abhorrent.

12. The Balfour Report, named for its author, Arthur Balfour (British Conservative Party Prime Minister, 1902-5), was a document agreed to during the Imperial Conference of 1926 in London. It recognized the independence of the "dominions" and therefore the validity of the idea of a Commonwealth. (Balfour was also the author of another report, one that in 1917 recommended to the British government that Palestine be established as a Jewish homeland.)

13. A phrase to which, as Chinua Achebe puts it, "an Indian would

reply: 'Yes, because God cannot trust an Englishman in the dark!'"
Home and Exile. New York: Oxford, 2000: 77.

14. It was, of course, always an artificial boundary, for critics in the field of "English-language Commonwealth literature" seldom — until the late 20th century — took into account the French-language literature of Canada; the Maori or Haida or other indigenous-language literatures of Canada, New Zealand, and other settler societies; or the literatures written in the many indigenous languages of Africa or South and Southeast Asia — even when the same writers (Ngugi wa Thiong'o, for one) wrote both in English and in another tongue (in Ngugi's case, Kikuyu). South African critics were a partial exception, for comparative studies of writings in English and Afrikaans did exist, although reference to literatures in Xhosa or Zulu remained scarce.

15. By no means was this the only British response. As Diana Athill, the longtime editor at Andre Deutsch, recalls in her memoir *Stet* (London: Granta, 2000), "Most of the people in our trade were more liberal than not, feeling guilty at being subjects of an imperial power and pleased that with the war's end Britain began relinquishing its so-called 'possessions' overseas. And many of them were genuinely interested in hearing what writers in those countries had to say now that they were free" (103).

16. *Colonial & Postcolonial Literature.* Oxford: Oxford UP, 1995: 158.

17. New York: St Martin's, 1956: 78.

18. Boehmer makes the point that even those who resisted colonial authority (to which one might add those whom class or race or gender marginalized at home) "were vulnerable to containment" (168). Writers might seek to "name the world for themselves," but legitimizing this search was fraught with challenges. Publishers could refuse to publish; readers could fail to read with sensitivity; "subversion" or "experiment" could be neutralized by silence as well as by open dismissal.

19. *WLWE* 30.2 (1990): 30-41.

20. The data in the following section is derived from Eric Williams, *From Columbus to Castro: The History of the Caribbean 1492-1962.* New York and Evanston: Harper & Row, 1970.

21. The Middle Passage came to be excoriated in Caribbean history, but also adapted in Caribbean literature as a forceful trope in its own right, to refer to the "voyage into slavery," whether in empirical or

metaphorical terms. Austin Clarke, for example, used the term to describe Caribbean emigration to Canada and entry into "domestic service," which is constructed as another version of slavery.

22. See Robin W. Winks, *The Blacks in Canada*. 2nd ed. Montreal: McGill-Queens UP, 1997; and Cecil Foster, *A Place Called Heaven*. Toronto: HarperCollins, 1996.

23. "Colonial Literatures," in *New National and Post-Colonial Literatures: An Introduction*, ed. Bruce King. Oxford: Clarendon, 1998: 110-11.

24. Introduction to *In the Castle of My Skin*. 1970; Ann Arbor, U Michigan P, 1991: xxxviii; qtd in "Colonial Literatures," 111.

25. *Roughing It in the Bush*. 1852; rpt Toronto: McClelland and Stewart, 1989: 40.

26. Rpt. Ottawa: Tecumseh, 1986; ed. Thomas E. Tausky.

27. New York: Grove Weidenfeld, 1989.

28. *The Circle Game;* rpt. in *Selected Poems*. Toronto: Oxford, 1976: 25.

29. *Jazz Waiata*. Auckland: Auckland UP, 1990. "Tai Tokerau" is the Maori name for the Bay of Islands, in northern New Zealand.

30. The contacts also resulted in a number of reformative fictions about, for example, Eurasian identities, as with Govind Desani's linguistically ebullient *All About H. Hatterr, A Gesture* (1948; New York: Farrar Straus & Young, 1951), where the energy of moving on takes precedence over the stasis of racial category. Many colonial writers during the 19th century, moreover, stretched, through plotline or metaphor, to articulate the cosmopolitan advantages of a mixed heritage, as when the Indian poet Toru Dutt sets up a quarrel between the lily and the rose as to which is more beautiful, resolving the dilemma by affirming the precedence of the bicoloured lotus ("The Lotus," *Ancient Ballads and Legends of Hindustan*. London: Kegan Paul, 1882: 136); or as when a score of writers of such fictions as Mrs. Humphrey Ward's *Canadian Born* (London: Smith Elder, 1910) wrap up everything by engaging a British or French or American parent with one of the others and producing a Canadian child as an embodiment of the future. The vocabulary of popular rhetoric — "two solitudes," for example — no matter that it is sometimes inaccurately transcribed and imperfectly applied, often reinforces such a view.

31. "A Far Cry from Africa" (*In a Green Night,* 1962), rpt. in *The Penguin Book of Caribbean Verse in English,* ed. Paula Burnett, Harmonds-

worth: Penguin, 1986: 243. By the time of his later "The Schooner *Flight*" (*The Star-Apple Kingdom*, 1979), Walcott presents in a different way this challenge to identity; here his multiracial character Shabine says of himself: "I have Dutch, nigger, and English in me, / and either I'm nobody, or I'm a nation" (rpt in John Figueroa, ed. *An Anthology of African and Caribbean Writing in English.* London: Heinemann Educational, 1982: 280). In Walcott's writing, affirmation does become possible, but it usually comes accompanied by some sort of loss.

32. Naipaul, "The Baker's Story," in John Figueroa: 106-13; Mittelholzer, *A Morning at the Office.* London: Hogarth, 1950.

33. *The Penguin Book of Modern African Poetry.* Ed. Gerald Moore and Ulli Beier. 3rd ed.; Harmondsworth: Penguin, 1986: 187.

34. *The Arrivants.* London: Oxford, 1973: 270.

35. Maya Deren, *The Voodoo Gods of Haiti.* London: Thames & Hudson, 1953: 61.

36. For example, Frye in *Anatomy of Criticism.*

37. Numerous postcolonial writings deal precisely with the fact that sometimes irony is *ineffective* against entrenched order: some systemized violence (such as that which uses a sectarian belief in racial "purity" as a way to justify and validate torture) is not immediately susceptible to critique, as is illustrated by Hugh Lewin's poem "Touch," written after the South African author's own seven years in prison, about the multiple constraints of imprisonment under an apartheid regime. In six irregular stanzas, Lewin's speaker rehearses the difference between touch and untouchability, between fists and paws and loving gestures, and by the end of the poem longs to learn "how life feels," to be able to say "Here I am / please touch me." (*Poets to the People,* ed. Barry Feinberg, London: Heinemann, 1974, enl. 1980; rpt. in *A New Book of South African Verse in English,* ed. Guy Butler and Chris Mann, Cape Town: Oxford, 1979.) One can read such a poem as a despairing cry, or also as an affirmation of a continuing faith in possibility; it may also be reasonable to argue that, for this speaker, the only comprehensible alternative to the existing punitive and discriminatory social "world of order" lies in language itself, in the intricate modulations of textual change that construct order in voice and on the page.

38. 1986; rpt. in *The Macmillan Anthology of Australian Literature.* Ed. Ken Goodwin and Alan Lawson. Melbourne: Macmillan, 1990: 14-15.

39. I know, too, that the Maori writer Witi Ihimaera, by turning Sydney into the Emerald City in *Pounamu, Pounamu* [greenstone, greenstone], ironically twists its meaning, representing the city's attractions as a material substitute for New Zealand jade, the "greenstone" that traditionally represented cultural value. Sydney of course *is* the largest Maori city in the world, but this is a "fact" a little like knowing that Los Angeles is the second (or is it third?) largest *Canadian* city in the world, the cohort of people who make it so composed entirely of those who (adapting Atwood's phrase "home ground, foreign territory") find themselves in foreign territory, perhaps succeeding in calling it home.

Home, of course, has been defined in different ways. The New Zealand writer Alan Mulgan wrote a book called *Home: A Colonial's Adventure* (London: Longmans, Green, 1927) — meaning a sojourn in London. And "Home" remained in London for many settler-colonists until they went, or went back, to see it for themselves. Some of Margaret Laurence's characters (such as Uncle Dan in "The Sound of the Singing," one of several stories where Vanessa MacLeod is coming to terms with her grandfather; in *A Bird in the House*. 1974; rpt Toronto: McClelland & Stewart, 1989) yearn for a Scotland or Ireland that they imagine as their past, only to discover that their Ireland is more in Ontario than in Europe, their Scotland a figment of romance. Other writers sought Utopia in new lands and depicted characters who could be disappointed or instructed by the land and its people (such as Catherine Helen Spence in *Handfasted,* which locates a Scots Utopia in the American West, run by women and affirming freedom from Presbyterian blame [complete but unpublished in 1880 because of what were considered its libertine views, the novel first appeared in 1984 from Penguin Publishers, Ringwood, Australia]; still other writers celebrated Arcadia by replanting the familiar in new territory, ignoring local realities, and aggrandizing themselves or their characters (such as William Pember Reeves in "A Colonist in his Garden" [from *New Zealand and Other Poems,* 1898; rpt in Robert Chapman and Jonathan Bennett, eds. *An Anthology of New Zealand Verse*. London and Wellington: Oxford, 1956: 37], where history apparently begins and ends with the colonist-settler and the chief ornament in his garden is his daughter, his "English rose"). One real-life irony, of course, is that Reeves, after celebrating why his "colonist" would stay forever in New

Zealand, himself packed up and went home to Britain to retire. His action represents a condition of inadaptability that much subsequent writing in the Commonwealth attempts through irony to resist.

40. As explained, for example, in Olive Patricia Dickason, *The Myth of the Savage*. Edmonton: U Alberta P, 1984.

41. Indeed, the Caribbean antipathy to "Daffodils" is practically endemic: it permeates works by Jamaica Kincaid, Michelle Cliff, and Erna Brodber as well, as in Kincaid, *Lucy*. New York: Farrrar Straus Giroux, 1990; Cliff, *No Telephone to Heaven*. New York: Dutton, 1987; Brodber, *Myal*. London: New Beacon, 1988. Naipaul's story appears in *Miguel Street*. London: Andre Deutsch, 1960.

42. Anonymous. Rpt in *The Macmillan Anthology of Australian Literature:* 247-8.

43. Bersianik, *L'Eugélionne*. Montréal: La Presse, 1976; translated 1981, 1996. One might argue that the short writings of Ania Walwicz and Anna Couani — as respectively in *Red Roses* (St. Lucia, Qld: U Queensland P, 1992) and *Italy; &, The train* (Clifton Hill, Vic.: Rigmarole Books, 1983) — perhaps come closest to deconstructing the conventional linguistic rules of English, in that they demonstrate in part how a sophisticated kind of communication can persist even when "sentences" are reduced to syllables, single words, and fragments.

44. For example, Brathwaite's "Rites," in *The Arrivants;* the vernacular passages that appear in the more formal context of Walcott's *Omeros;* the several revised versions of Moorehouse's "The Drover's Wife"; or Dawe's "Life-Cycle," told through the language of rugby.

45. *Down the Line*. Singapore: Heinemann Asia, 1980: 16.

46. Curnow, in Chapman and Bennett 153-4; Bennett, in Burnett 33; Ghose, in *The Violent West* 56-7.

47. *The Violent West*. London: Macmillan, 1972: 56-7.

48. *Stony Plain*. Erin, ON: Press Porcépic, 1973: 64; based on the transition table in Ernest H. Winter's *Learning to Write*, 2nd ed., rev. Toronto: Macmillan, 1961: 156.

49. "English in India." In John Press, ed., *Commonwealth Literature*. London: Heinemann Educational, 1965: 120-1.

50. "The Novelist as Teacher." In John Press, ed.: 201-5.

51. *Touch Mi Tell Mi* (Bogle L'Ouverture Publications); rpt in *Literature in English*. Ed. W.H. New and W.E. Messenger. Scarborough:

Prentice-Hall Canada, 1993: 1537.

52. *Mangoes & Bullets*. London and Sydney: Pluto, 1985: 44.

53. Some readers may be more familiar with this figure through Michael Ondaatje's allusion to her in his poem sequence *The man with seven toes* (1969).

54. *A Fringe of Leaves*. Rpt. Harmondsworth: Penguin, 1985: 7-8.

55. "Irony Is Not Enough: Essay on My Life as Catherine Deneuve," *Seneca R* 27.2 (1997): 35.

56. *Hunting the Wild Pineapple*. 1979; rpt. Ringwood, Victoria: Penguin, 1985: 175.

INDEX